D0841931

Simply Delicious

SUNDAY DINNERS

Fresh **52** *Recipes*

HOMESTYLE

PRAISE FOR *Simply Delicious Sunday Dinners*

"With *Simply Delicious Sunday Dinners*, Dina Foglio Crowell is helping bring back the classic Sunday dinner. Her fuss-free, homey recipes, like barbacoa, carrot slaw, and peach cobbler, will make the family table the place to be, week after week."

— Ellie Martin Cliffe
Senior editor, *Taste of Home* and *Simple & Delicious* magazines

"Mom's Sweet Sausage Baked Beans, Creamy Chicken Tomato Stew, and Jalapeño Popper Mac and Cheese are just a few of many supreme, savory dishes created by Dina. Easy, simple, and delicious, these are perfect everyday meals for your everyday family!"

— recipechart.com

Simply Delicious

SUNDAY DINNERS

Fresh **52** *Recipes*

•HOMESTYLE•

DINA FOGLIO CROWELL

Author of *Delicious Mornings*
and popular food blog
www.buttercream-bakehouse.com

FRONT TABLE BOOKS | AN IMPRINT OF CEDAR FORT, INC. | SPRINGVILLE, UTAH

ISBN 13: 978-1-4621-1764-2

Published by Front Table Books, an imprint of Cedar Fort, Inc.
2373 W. 700 S., Springville, UT 84663
Distributed by Cedar Fort, Inc., www.cedarfort.com

LIBRARY OF CONGRESS CATALOGING-IN-PUBLICATION DATA

Crowell, Dina Foglio, 1974- author.
Simply delicious Sunday dinners : 52 fresh homestyle recipes / Dina Foglio Crowell.
    pages cm
Includes index.
ISBN 978-1-4621-1764-2 (layflat binding : alk. paper)
1. Dinners and dining. I. Title.
TX737.C77 2015
641.5'4--dc23
                            2015033383

Cover and page design by M. Shaun McMurdie
Cover design © 2016 by Lyle Mortimer
Edited by Melissa J. Caldwell

Printed in China

10 9 8 7 6 5 4 3 2 1

Printed on acid-free paper

To my precious kiddos!

Thank you for sacrificing your time with me so that I could work on this project. The mommy guilt really got to me this time around but with all of the effort, energy, and hard work that went into this project, what remains is a priceless treasure. This cookbook is filled with family recipes from both my childhood and yours. I hope that when you are older, you'll cherish this book because it is filled with love, laughter, and wonderful memories. Now sit down and eat your dinner!

Love you all so much,

Mom

CONTENTS

HOMESTYLE FAVORITE BEEF DINNERS

WARM YOU UP SOUPS AND STEWS

FRESH HOMEMADE SIDES

FAMILY FAVORITE DESSERTS

ABOUT THE AUTHOR *144*

ACKNOWLEDGMENTS

These recipes did not magically appear. If it were not for receiving untiring support, encouragement and positive refocusing from my family and friends, then this book would not have come to be. Thank you to those who gently critiqued my photography for the book, taste-tested the recipes, offered cooking vessels or props for my photo shoots, and kept me going when I didn't think I had anything left in me. Cooking has a greater personal reward when the meal is over. My kids smile and say, "That was a good one, Mom. You should put that in your book!"

Buttercream Bakehouse is where I began. My love for baking, sharing cooking tips, and inspiration to create recipes is showcased on my little blog of love where you'll find me most often. I thank each of you for allowing me to come into your kitchens virtually through your steady readership and faithful following. The camaraderie of foodies and support from my readers is why I do what I do.

To my amazing friends who offer their advice and share their unbiased view and critiques on Facebook when I upload yet another food picture for the book, I thank you. Your opinions and thoughtful comments about my photography helped me select the food photos that made the cut for this book. Comments like "the plate was beautiful," "that hamburger looks so juicy, I want some!" and my all-time favorite, "OMG that looks so good, I want to put my face in that!" all meant that my food and photos were darn good and I was on a roll. So, I thank you!

To some very special and dear friends (you know who you are), I thank you for the priceless gift of friendship, love, encouragement, and continued support you have shown me without boundaries. It truly does "take a village," and I appreciate you more than you will ever know.

Most important to my children, Tristen, Ashlynn, Kayeden, and Brennen, who never tire of Mom's cooking or baking experiments. My sweet little Maltese, Ollie and Finn, who love the scraps, the mess-ups, or leftovers and are forever cuddling at my feet while I sit at my computer editing photos and typing away. To my adoring parents, Lucy and Jimmy Foglio, for their unconditional love, support, and encouragement. To Andria Post, a foodie at heart, thank you for offering your supportive talents and critiques.

From the bottom of my heart, I thank all of you!

INTRODUCTION

My childhood is full of memories of storytelling and sibling shenanigans around the dinner table. We were a busy bunch, just like most families, but on the weekends, **especially Sundays**, we managed to sit down together at the dinner table and enjoy a home-cooked meal. My parents both sat at either end of the table while my brothers sat across from me. I usually sat closest to my Mom because I knew she would protect me from my brothers. I was the middle child and only girl so you can imagine the fun they had with me. Whether they were flicking morsels of food at my face, touching my plate with their dirty fingers, or blowing on my food to see what I would do, there was always something happening at the table. Between each bite my Mom demanded they stop and eat their food while my Dad tirelessly chimed in with stories of his boyhood mischief as my brothers and I managed to settle down and quietly relish every bite. And the food—it was delicious.

When I was growing up, my Dad was a hardworking man with little time to himself. No matter how busy he was, he always made time to cook for his family. On Sundays he would make a fabulous dinner from scratch. He would get up early in the morning to boil the chicken needed to make his delicious chicken noodle soup (page 89).

Hovering over the kitchen sink, he would tirelessly shred the chicken between his fingers, cautiously making effort to keep the chicken a very fine texture. A true labor of love! Then he tossed in vegetables and seasonings and let it simmer all day. While it simmered, Dad tended to whatever needed fixing around the house, or tinkered in the garage on one of the vehicles. But he never lost his focus. He took frequent breaks to baby his boiling pot of liquid gold, adding a touch more of this and a tad more of that until it was an original masterpiece!

Dad has a delicate palate and can re-create recipes that he enjoys. He was absolutely spot on when re-creating my Grandma Foglio's sauce (Foglio Sunday Sauce, page 33) that she made for him growing up and now I share with you. My Grandma Foglio was a great Italian cook. She made her own pasta and strung it around the kitchen to dry while her sauce, the preeminent of all sauces, bubbled to perfection on the stove. It was a hearty, savory sauce with authentic Italian flavor. Like nothing you could ever order in a restaurant or that came out of a jar. It was made with love and is simply priceless. To this day, the aroma of homemade meatballs cooking reminds me of my childhood in Burke, Virginia, where I grew up.

My Dad was the dinner guru while my Mom loved to bake desserts and invent delicious side dishes that she is well-known for. During the summer months, my daughter often requested that her Grammy make her favorite, macaroni salad (page 127) while friends and neighbors fall to their knees for her **Perfect Potato Salad** (page 126).

The recipes in this cookbook have been in our family for decades. I remember the excitement of scooping spoonfuls of Mom's side dishes on my plate. The one that I loved most, and still do, is Mom's Sweet

Sausage Baked Beans (page 118). It has that sweet/heat combination from the brown sugar, molasses, and red pepper flakes that I love so much. You will notice the sweet/heat combination repeatedly in this book and Mom's Sweet Sausage Baked Beans is what shaped my palate to crave this complex flavor explosion.

This recipe is still requested by friends and family who remember it being so enticing and delicious years ago. "Bring your mom's baked beans!" is something I hear quite often, and now I am sharing this fabulous side dish with you.

My mom was also a hard worker. With both my parents working two jobs each, we became latchkey kids in a hurry. When we would come home from school, Mom would occasionally leave homemade cookies or brownies waiting for us, something I will always remember. My parents took the time to fill our tummies with love as I do now for my own kiddos.

I picked up on my parents' love for food at a young age. As a child I loved to experiment in the kitchen and discovered my first love: baking desserts. When I was an adult and started my own family, everything was centered around food. I planned for every meal each day of the week. I created every party and holiday menu with new recipes and old favorites too. When I baked and decorated my son's first birthday cake, I knew I had a knack for making food that looked as great as it tasted. As my love for baking and creating grew, I wanted to inspire others to try something new and simple to create, so I decided to share my passion and my recipes with the world. In 2010, I started my own baking blog called Buttercream Bakehouse (www.buttercreambakehouse.com) to do just that.

As my blog grew in popularity, I secured my first book deal. In 2014 a dream came true: my first cookbook, *Delicious Mornings,* was released. It has been a whirlwind since I became a published author and now here I am, releasing my second book. With my new dinner cookbook I can continue to share fabulous recipes that are easy to prepare and taste out of this world.

This book is special to me because each recipe is made with love, which is something I learned from my parents. I aim to prepare quality home-style meals for my family and yours that can be enjoyed together sitting at the table when possible. There is nothing more memorable and meaningful than sitting with your family and reconnecting over a delicious homestyle dinner and the flavors you created for them. In our home that means our cell phones are put away, the dogs are by our side begging for scraps, and the kids are chattering about their days. . . . Or sometimes throwing morsels of food at each other and creating their own havoc and childhood memories.

In this book, you will discover original family favorites along with modern recipes such as Jalapeño Popper Mac and Cheese (page 45) or Cheeseburger Casserole (page 49), scrumptious side dishes that are fresh and exciting, and delectable desserts that are real crowd pleasers. All with simple, easy-to-find ingredients and some time-saving tips that will help you create a homestyle meal for your family that you can be proud of. "Seconds please!" is music to my ears and I know my job is done. ***Bon appetito*! It's time to eat!**

COOKING GLOSSARY

Here are some basic cooking terms used throughout this cookbook. Knowing these terms will help you understand the cooking directions in this cookbook, which will help you prepare your meal with ease. Happy cooking!

FOOD PREPARATION METHODS

Bake	Cooking food using dry heat without direct exposure to a flame, typically in an oven
Blanch	A cooking process where the food is plunged into boiling water, removed after a brief timed interval, and then plunged into ice water to halt the cooking process
Chop	Cut with a knife or food processor into smaller pieces
Crush	Smash into smaller pieces, generally using hands, a mortar and pestle, or a rolling pin (crushing dried herbs releases their flavor and aroma)
Dice	Cut in small cubes of the same size and shape
Pitted	Removed the seed from fruit
Preheat	Heat an oven or a utensil to a specific temperature before using it
Roast	Cook a large piece of meat or poultry uncovered with dry heat in an oven
Sauté	Cooking and stirring food in a small amount of fat over fairly high heat in an open, shallow pan
Simmer	Cook food in a liquid that is kept just below the boiling point; a liquid is simmering when a few bubbles form slowly and burst just before reaching the surface
Tenderize	Pounding or piercing meat to break down collagens in the meat to make it more palatable and tender
Whisk	Beat ingredients (such as heavy or whipping cream, eggs, salad dressings, or sauces) with a fork or whisk to mix or incorporate air

COOKING TOOLS

Blender	A stationary electric mixing machine with a rotating blade used for liquefying, chopping, or pureeing food
Casserole dish	A large, deep dish used both in the oven and as a serving vessel. Can be oval, square, or rectangular, and either glass, ceramic, or stone
Cookie sheet	A flat metal tray for baking in the oven. Can be rectangular or circle
Dutch oven	A large, heavy cooking pot with a lid for cooking meats, stews, and soups
Garlic press	A kitchen utensil used to crush garlic cloves by forcing it through a grid of small holes
Meat tenderizer	A mallet used to pierce and pound meat to make it tender and easy to eat
Saucepan	A cooking vessel used on the stove for heating food. Typically aluminum, stainless steel, or Teflon
Skillet	A flat-bottomed pan used for frying, searing, and browning foods
Slow cooker	A large electric pot used for slow cooking food, especially stews and meat
Wire whisk	A cooking utensil to blend ingredients smooth or to incorporate air into a mixture

Note: *Salt and Fresh Cracked Black Pepper, to Taste*

In this cookbook you will often notice that recipes call for "salt and fresh cracked black pepper, to taste." What does this mean? In a nutshell, this means to season the dish according to your palate. Salt, when used properly, brings out the natural flavor in food. How do you know what is correct if there is no measurement in the recipe? That's basically up to you and your palate in preparing your recipe. To me, a teaspoon of salt is nothing, but to some it could be overkill. Just remember, you are not trying to "taste" the salt or make a dish salty to taste. You want the salt to enhance the natural flavor or the dish. Same goes for fresh cracked black pepper. Simply add a pinch of salt at a time; then taste and adjust the flavor to suit your palate. I invite you to be creative with *all* of your seasonings and to make the dish your own. Also, try and use fresh cracked black pepper when possible. Your taste buds will thank you. Happy cooking!

CHICKEN, PORK CHOPS, AND LAMB

Come and get it!

Simple and delicious homestyle entrées that will please even your pickiest eaters. Whether it's sautéed, baked, slow cooked, or roasted, these recipes are easy to prepare and packed with flavor.

STICKY SOY CHICKEN *with* ASIAN CARROT SLAW

SERVES 6-8

This dish is finger lickin' good and keeps you wanting more. When baked, the honey caramelizes into sticky, sweet goodness that blends seamlessly with the garlic and soy sauce. Goes great with white rice and Asian Carrot Slaw (page 112).

12–15 chicken drumsticks and thighs

salt and fresh cracked black pepper, to taste

2 Tbsp. sesame oil

2 Tbsp. ketchup

½ cup soy sauce

½ cup pure honey

2 cloves garlic, minced

½ cup green scallions, thinly sliced

Preheat oven to 400 degrees. Wash and dry 12–15 chicken drumsticks and thighs. Place in a 9 × 13-inch glass baking dish. Season lightly with salt and fresh cracked black pepper to taste. Remember that soy sauce is super salty, so go easy here.

For the marinade, using a wire whisk, combine the remaining ingredients in a small bowl, except for the green scallions. If you don't have a garlic press to mince the garlic, chop the garlic into small, fine pieces. Pour marinade over chicken. Turn chicken with your hands or tongs. Arrange skin-side down in the baking dish. Bake for 30 minutes. Remove pan, turn chicken over, and sprinkle with green onions. Bake for another 30–45 minutes until meat is a golden brown and is falling off the bone.

MAKE AHEAD: *This dish can be prepared the night before. Simply assemble the uncooked chicken in the glass baking dish with marinade. Cover and refrigerate until the next day. Bake within 24 hours.*

ULTIMATE SLOW COOKER TURKEY BREAST

SERVES 8-10

Cooked turkey breast often becomes too dry. This recipe solves that problem pronto! A slow cooker naturally bastes the turkey while it cooks, and adding chicken broth boosts the moistness to produce a succulent, tender turkey with ultimate flavor. I like to serve my turkey alongside Roasted Asparagus with Lemon and Parmesan (page 109) and Jalapeño Cranberry Salsa (page 113).

3–5 lbs. turkey breast

1 Tbsp. extra virgin olive oil

salt and fresh cracked black pepper, to taste

1 Tbsp. dried sage

2 Tbsp. dried rosemary

1 Tbsp. dried thyme

1 Tbsp. paprika

1 yellow onion, sliced

5–6 garlic cloves

1 (14-oz.) can chicken broth

Rinse turkey breast under cold water. Pat dry with paper towel. Rub turkey breast with extra virgin olive oil all over. Sprinkle turkey breast with a generous amount of salt and fresh cracked black pepper and herbs. Sprinkle all over with paprika. This will keep the skin from getting soggy and add extra flavor. Add onions and garlic around turkey, placing a few garlic cloves underneath the skin. Pour entire can of chicken broth into slow cooker, but not on top of turkey breast. Close lid and cook on high for 5 hours or until tender. Remove from slow cooker, slice, and serve warm with turkey gravy.

COOKING TIP: *You can exchange the extra virgin olive oil for butter and substitute the dried herbs for fresh herbs. If using fresh herbs, loosen the skin gently and tuck fresh herb sprigs underneath.*

SHERRY CHICKEN DIVAN *with* BABY BELLA MUSHROOMS

SERVES 6-8

When company comes, this is a great dish to serve. The baby bella mushrooms in this recipe give it an earthy texture and flavor while the sherry brings a sophisticated note to the classic chicken divan. Add a baguette and a side of rice to soak up all the lovely sauce.

2 chicken breasts

extra virgin olive oil

salt and fresh cracked black pepper, to taste

1 cup yellow onion, diced

1½ cups petite baby bella mushrooms

5 Tbsp. butter, divided

1½ cups cooked broccoli (if frozen, thawed)

3 Tbsp. flour

1½ cups half-and-half

¾ cup heavy cream

⅔ cup mayonnaise

2 Tbsp. Worcestershire sauce

1 tsp. curry powder

3 Tbsp. dry sherry

1 (10.5-oz.) can condensed celery soup

1 cup shredded Parmesan cheese

2–3 slices fresh bread, grounded to fine crumbs in food processor

2 Tbsp. melted butter

Preheat oven to 400 degrees. Sauté chicken in frying pan with extra virgin olive oil. Season both sides with salt and fresh cracked black pepper. Remove from pan and cut chicken into 1-inch cubes. Sauté onions and mushrooms with 2 tablespoons butter. Remove from pan and add to chicken. Add thawed broccoli. Set aside.

In a large saucepan on medium heat, whisk together 3 tablespoons of butter and flour until smooth thick paste. Add half-and-half and cream, and whisk until butter and flour mixture is completely smooth and liquid is lump free. Add mayonnaise, Worcestershire sauce, curry, sherry, and celery soup, and stir until heated and bubbly and thoroughly combined. Pour mixture over chicken and toss to coat. Sprinkle top evenly with shredded Parmesan cheese and bread crumbs. Drizzle with melted butter. Add salt and fresh cracked black pepper to taste.

SIMPLE SKILLET PORK CHOPS

SERVES 4

I like my pork chops simple: juicy and lightly seasoned with salt and fresh cracked black pepper, and cooked in a little extra virgin olive oil. The pork chops are first seared on high heat to form a golden outer crust. Then the heat is lowered and the pan is covered to ensure a tender juicy center. I love pork chops with apples so I like to serve this entree with Country Fried Apples (page 119) and Garlic Mashed Potatoes (page 110).

---

4 thick bone-in pork loin chops

salt and fresh cracked black pepper, to taste

3–4 Tbsp. extra virgin olive oil

Remove pork chops from refrigerator and let sit at room temperature for 30 minutes. Drizzle extra virgin olive oil in a large skillet and turn heat to high. Sprinkle each pork chop on both sides with salt and fresh cracked black pepper, and cook on high heat on each side for 1 minute until golden brown. This golden outer crust will give great flavor and help seal in moisture. Lower heat to medium and cover skillet with a lid. Cook an additional 4 minutes per side, turning once. Remove from heat and let pork chops rest for ten more minutes to seal in juices.

OVEN "FRIED" CHICKEN LEGS

SERVES 6-8

This recipe has the same ingredients as typical fried chicken but it is baked rather than fried, making it healthier for you and faster to prepare. Save the messy frying for someone else; this tasty lightly seasoned "fried" chicken is sure to become a family favorite.

2 eggs, beaten

½ cup whole milk

2 cups cornflakes, crushed in food processor

1 tsp. parsley

2 tsp. Italian seasoning

½ tsp. paprika

½ tsp. salt

½ tsp. fresh cracked black pepper

12–15 pieces chicken legs

Preheat oven to 375 degrees. In a small bowl, combine egg and milk. In a food processor or blender, crush the cornflakes to a medium crumb. In a large dish, toss cornflakes and seasonings. Rinse and dry chicken legs. One at a time, dip chicken legs in egg mixture and then roll directly into crumb mixture, coating all sides.

Line a large cookie sheet with foil. Spray with cooking spray. Arrange chicken legs so they are not touching on pan.

Sprinkle remaining cornflake mixture onto legs to ensure a generous coating.

Bake uncovered for 45–55 minutes or until chicken is no longer pink.

CHICKEN COBBLER PIE

SERVES 4-6

Tender pieces of chicken and chunky vegetables baked in seasoned creamy chicken gravy and encased in a buttery, flakey crust. This is the ultimate in comfort food. Serve with a salad and biscuits, and you'll be getting lots of hugs by the end of the meal. Enjoy!

---

3 boneless chicken breasts

3 Tbsp. extra virgin olive oil for cooking

3 Tbsp. butter

1 cup mushrooms, washed and sliced

½ cup celery, sliced

⅓ cup onion, diced

½ cup flour

2 cups chicken stock

1 cup half-and-half

1 chicken bouillon cube

1½ cups frozen green peas and carrots, thawed

½ tsp. salt

¼ tsp. fresh cracked black pepper

¼ tsp. celery salt

2 (9-inch) unbaked pie crusts

Preheat oven to 400 degrees. Line a 9-inch deep dish pie plate with one pie crust. Press the sides firmly up to the edge of pie plate. Set aside second pie crust.

Using a meat tenderizer, pound chicken breasts on both sides. Salt and pepper chicken to taste and cook with olive oil in a large frying pan on medium-high heat, turning once. Cook until juices run clear 8–12 minutes. Remove from pan.

In same pan, add butter and sauté the mushrooms, celery, and onions until soft and onions are translucent, 4–5 minutes.

Using a wire whisk, whisk in flour and gradually stir in chicken stock, half and half, and chicken bouillon, stirring until mixture is bubbly, thickened, and lump free.

Stir in chicken and peas and carrots. Add salt, fresh cracked black pepper, and celery salt. Remove from heat. Spoon chicken mixture into crust-lined pan. Top with second crust and seal edge by pinching crust between two fingers or using a fork to press securely. Cut slits in several places on top crust.

Bake 40 minutes or until crust is golden brown. If edges are browning too quickly, simply cover with strips of foil during the last 15 minutes of baking. Let stand 5 minutes before serving.

CREAMY WHITE WINE CHICKEN *and* BISCUITS *with* PIMENTO

SERVES 6-8

The perfect comfort food in one amazing casserole! Tender chicken, melted cheese, and golden, buttery biscuits all baked in a creamy, rich pimento white wine sauce that tastes fabulous over white rice. Add a Homemade Caesar Salad (page 123) or Ashlynn's Ambrosia Salad (page 116) for a complete homestyle country meal.

4 chicken breasts

salt and fresh cracked black pepper

2 Tbsp. extra virgin olive oil

4 Tbsp. butter, melted and divided

½ large onion, chopped

2 (10.75-oz.) cans cream of chicken soup

½ cup sour cream

1 cup milk

1 (4-oz.) jar pimentos with juice

1 tsp. dried thyme

½ tsp. dried parsley

¼ cup dry white wine

1 cup shredded mild cheddar cheese, divided

6 frozen biscuits, thawed

Preheat oven to 350 degrees. Grease a 7 × 11 baking dish with cooking spray.

Using a meat tenderizer, pound 4 chicken breasts on both sides. Sprinkle salt and fresh cracked black pepper on the chicken. In a large skillet, cook chicken with olive oil until no longer pink. Remove chicken and cool slightly. In same skillet, melt 2 tablespoons butter on medium heat. Cook onion until translucent, 4–5 minutes. Shred or cube the chicken, add to skillet, and toss to warm. In a medium mixing bowl, combine the chicken soup, sour cream, milk, pimentos, thyme, parsley, and white wine until combined. Add to chicken and onion mixture and stir. Pour into prepared baking dish.

Bake in preheated oven until chicken and sauce are hot and bubbly, 15 minutes. Remove from oven and sprinkle top with shredded cheddar cheese. Arrange biscuits in a single layer on top of cheese. Using a pastry brush, brush biscuits with remaining 2 tablespoons melted butter and return to oven. Bake for an additional 20 minutes or until biscuits are golden browned and cooked through. The biscuits will cook faster if they are not touching. Serve over rice.

FIVE-SPICE CHICKEN *with* CHERRY BASIL SALSA

SERVES 4

You've probably noticed that I am a lover of all things spicy and sweet. This recipe is a true testament to that. The Chinese five spice powder gives a unique flavor to the tender, moist chicken topped with a fiery hot jalapeño salsa made with tart cherries and basil. Spoon it right over your chicken for a delectable bite of flavorful goodness.

CHERRY BASIL SALSA

2 cups sweet cherries, pitted and chopped

1 jalapeño, seeded and finely chopped

⅓ cup finely chopped red onion

¼ cup fresh basil leaves, chopped

2 Tbsp. honey

¼ cup lemon juice

½ tsp. salt

¼ tsp. fresh cracked black pepper

FIVE-SPICE CHICKEN

4 chicken breasts

salt and fresh cracked black pepper, to taste

2 Tbsp. Chinese five-spice powder

2 Tbsp. extra virgin olive oil

To make the salsa, combine the cherries, jalapeño, red onion, basil, honey, lemon juice, salt, and fresh cracked black pepper in a small bowl. Set aside.

Rinse and dry chicken. On a flat surface, pound chicken with a meat tenderizer on both sides. Sprinkle lightly with salt and fresh cracked black pepper. Then season with Chinese five spice powder evenly over all four chicken breasts on both sides.

In a large skillet, add olive oil. Add chicken and cook for 5 minutes on medium heat. Turn chicken over and cook another 5 minutes or until lightly golden brown and juices run clear. Serve with cherry basil salsa over top.

SEASONED LAMB PITAS *with* MINT TZATZIKI SAUCE

SERVES 4

A simple and speedy version of a classic gyro sandwich but without all the fuss. Seasoned ground lamb has the same classic gyro flavors tucked into a store-bought pita and topped with a fabulous homemade Tzatziki sauce made with Dijon mustard, extra virgin olive oil, and red bell pepper.

SEASONED LAMB

1 Tbsp. vegetable oil

1 lb. ground lamb

½ cup white onion, diced

1 tsp. dried parsley

1 tsp. dried oregano

salt and fresh cracked black pepper, to taste

TZATZIKI SAUCE

½ cup plain yogurt

juice of 1 lemon

2 Tbsp. fresh mint, chopped

1 small garlic clove, minced

1 Tbsp. extra virgin olive oil

2 tsp. Dijon mustard

1 red fresh bell pepper, finely diced

4 pieces pita bread

1 cucumber, sliced thin

3 green scallions, sliced thin

In a large saucepan, heat vegetable oil on medium high heat. Add lamb and, while cooking, break up into small pieces and cook until no longer pink. Add onion and sauté with lamb until soft, two minutes. Add parsley, oregano, and salt and fresh cracked black pepper, and stir. Drain lamb in colander and return to pan to keep warm.

To make the Tzatziki sauce, add yogurt, lemon juice, mint, garlic, extra virgin olive oil, mustard, and red bell pepper in a small bowl and mix thoroughly.

Slice the top of a piece of pita bread and gently tuck in cooked lamb, cucumber slices, and scallions. Top with a heaping tablespoon or two of Tzatziki sauce. Serve lamb warm.

SWEET MESQUITE–BBQ WHOLE ROASTED CHICKEN

SERVES 4-6

Turn a whole roasted chicken into a backyard barbecue feast by using a sweet mesquite dry rub and delicious hickory brown sugar barbecue sauce to flavor your bird. If you can't find the sauce and rub I used for this recipe, use your favorite brand and flavor. Serve with corn on the cob and Mom's Sweet Sausage Baked Beans (page 118) for a true barbecue feast.

---

1 (3-lb.) whole chicken

salt and fresh cracked black pepper, to taste

sweet mesquite BBQ chicken dry rub (I used A1®)

Hickory brown sugar BBQ sauce (I used Jack Daniels®)

2 white onions, sliced thick

Rinse chicken well and remove giblets. Place the chicken on a clean countertop or cutting board, and pat it dry with paper towels.

Season generously inside and out with salt, pepper, and a mesquite BBQ–flavored dry rub. Using a pastry brush, brush entire chicken with hickory brown sugar BBQ sauce. Reserve some sauce for serving. Stuff sliced onions inside of chicken cavity as far back as it will go.

Roast the chicken in the oven for 15 minutes at 425 degrees. Reduce the temperature to 375 degrees and continue roasting until the juices run clear and a thermometer inserted into the inner thigh (but not touching the bone) registers 165 degrees, 50–60 minutes or more.

Remove the chicken from the oven and place on a cutting board. Let it rest 15–20 minutes before slicing. Serve with additional BBQ sauce if desired.

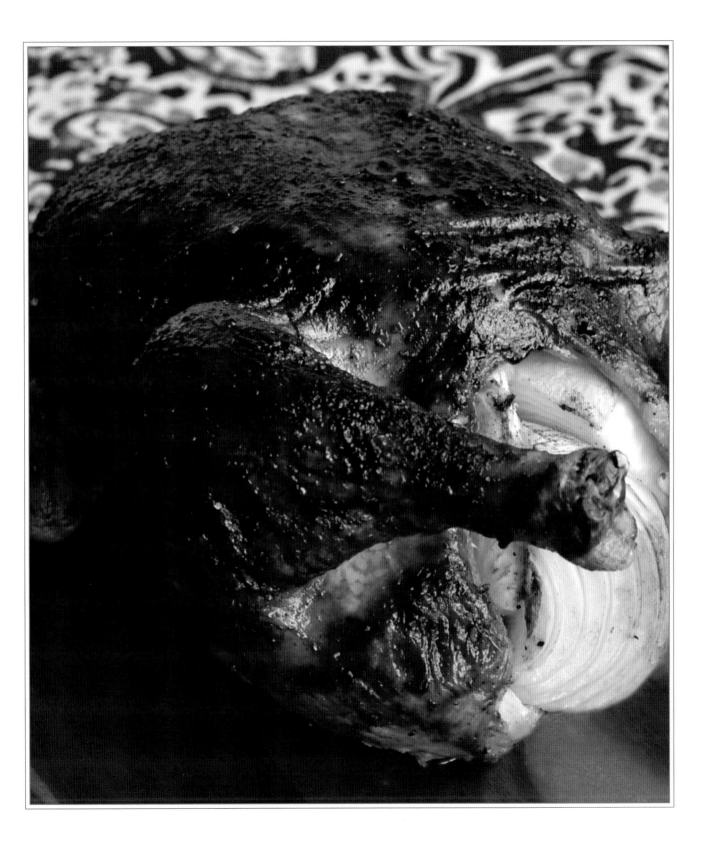

CITRUS CHICKEN

SERVES 4-6

This fragrant lightly sweetened citrus marinade has a fresh, bright flavor that makes the chicken not only tasty but super juicy and falling off the bone.

2 lemons, divided

2 oranges, divided

2 Tbsp. brown sugar

¼ cup extra virgin olive oil

1 tsp. oregano

¼ tsp. ground mustard

¼ tsp. salt

¼ tsp. fresh cracked black pepper

½ tsp. red pepper flakes

4 garlic cloves

1 small red onion, thinly sliced

1 Tbsp. fresh rosemary

10–12 chicken thighs and legs

Preheat oven to 400 degrees.

In a small bowl, juice 1 lemon and 1 orange. Whisk in the rest of the ingredients except onion and rosemary, until well blended. This makes the marinade.

Place chicken evenly in a rimmed 13×9 baking dish. Cover chicken with marinade, turning pieces to coat all sides. Cover and refrigerate for 30 minutes or up to two hours, if desired. Slice the remaining lemon and orange. Arrange slices of lemon, orange, and red onion on top of the chicken, tucking it under and beside chicken pieces. Sprinkle with rosemary and additional salt and fresh cracked black pepper if desired.

Bake uncovered for 1 hour or until chicken is cooked and juices run clear.

SWEAT PEACH BALSAMIC PORK CHOPS

SERVES 4-5

A simple peach and balsamic glaze adds a punch of sweetness to juicy succulent stove-top pork chops. Add wild rice and Tender Garlic Green Beans (page 125) for an amazing meal your family will devour.

---

2 tsp. extra virgin olive oil

5 bone-in pork chops (1 inch thick; 2½ lbs. total)

salt and fresh cracked black pepper

1 tsp. fresh rosemary, chopped

1 cup peach preserves

2 Tbsp. balsamic vinegar

Heat the olive oil in a large skillet over medium-high heat. Season the pork chops with a generous amount of salt and fresh cracked black pepper. Cook until browned and cooked through, 6–8 minutes per side. Sprinkle with rosemary.

In a small bowl, mix the peach preserves and balsamic vinegar until combined. Pour over cooked pork chops to coat and cook an additional 2 minutes. Serve with wild rice.

SLOW COOKER SHREDDED BBQ CHICKEN SANDWICHES

SERVES 8-10

I have been using this delicious pulled BBQ chicken sandwich recipe for years. I typically make it in the summer months. The meat is so tender and juicy and full of great BBQ flavor with a hint of pineapple.

2½ lbs. chicken breasts

1 package McCormick® Slow Cookers BBQ Pulled Pork Seasoning

¾ cup ketchup

½ cup brown sugar

⅓ cup apple cider vinegar

½ cup water

1 (8.25-oz.) can crushed pineapple

Place chicken in slow cooker. Mix seasoning, ketchup, brown sugar, vinegar, water, and pineapple until blended. Pour over chicken. Cover.

Cook 5 hours on low or 2½ hours on high.

In slow cooker, shred chicken using 2 forks. Mix and let chicken absorb juices. Serve on hamburger rolls.

SIMPLE PASTAS AND SEAFOOD

*Some of the easiest and tastiest meals are pasta and
seafood dishes. Using fresh herbs and vegetables is all it takes
to make a simple meal that is quick to assemble
and that your family will love.*

ROASTED RED PEPPER *and* FENNEL BAKED ROTINI

SERVES 4-6

Your family will love the pungent red pepper flavor and Italian sausage baked with the slightly sweet taste of fennel in this fabulous baked rotini.

---

1 (12-oz.) box rotini

3 Italian sausage patties, thawed

½ cup onion, diced

2 garlic cloves, minced

1 jar prepared spaghetti sauce
(I used Prego®)

3 Tbsp. jarred roasted red pepper, chopped

fresh cracked black pepper, to taste

2 cups mozzarella cheese

1 Tbsp. fennel seeds

1 tsp. Italian seasoning

Preheat oven to 375 degrees. Cook noodles according to package directions for al dente. Drain pasta and place back into pot it was cooked in.

In a large saucepan, add Italian sausage and cook for 3 minutes, breaking up into small pieces. Add onions and garlic and continue to cook until onions are translucent. Drain off excess grease from mixture and toss into pot with pasta. Add sauce and peppers and stir to combine. Add to a 13 × 9 casserole dish. Top with cheese, fennel, and Italian seasoning.

Bake uncovered for 25 minutes or until bubbly and cheese is melted and lightly golden brown.

CHICKEN PASTA SALAD *with* ARTICHOKE *and* ASPARAGUS

SERVES 8-10

Adding protein to pasta salad is a great way to turn a light meal into something amazing for dinner. Serve this with Farm Fresh Fruit Salad (page 115) and rolls for a light and healthy meal that is just as tasty and delicious as it looks.

---

3 chicken breasts

salt and fresh cracked black pepper for chicken breasts

2 Tbsp. extra virgin olive oil

1 bunch (12) asparagus spears, ends removed and cut in 2-inch pieces

1 (14-oz.) can artichoke hearts, drained and rinsed

1 Tbsp. lemon juice + 1 tsp. lemon zest

2 tsp. garlic, minced

2 Tbsp. butter

2 Tbsp. flour

2 cups milk

1 (8-oz.) box bow-tie pasta, cooked according to package directions

salt and fresh cracked black pepper, to taste

freshly grated Parmesan cheese

Pound chicken with a meat tenderizer on both sides. Lightly salt and pepper chicken, and cook in a large saucepan in extra virgin olive oil, turning often until juices run clear and lightly golden, 7 minutes.

While chicken is cooking, blanch asparagus by adding to a large pot of boiling water. Boil for 2 minutes until bright green. Rinse in colander under cold water to stop the cooking process.

Spray a large skillet with cooking spray. Add artichoke hearts, lemon juice, and lemon zest and cook over medium-high heat for 5 minutes. Add asparagus and cook another 2–4 minutes until tender, stirring often. Remove artichokes and asparagus with a slotted spoon and set aside.

Add butter and garlic to pan and stir for 1 minute until garlic is fragrant. Add flour and stir until mixture comes together, forming a ball. Slowly whisk in milk until smooth.

Add pasta and stir to coat. Stir in artichokes and asparagus. Season with salt and fresh cracked black pepper to taste and top with Parmesan cheese.

ANGEL HAIR PASTA *with* FRESH BASIL MARINARA

SERVES 3-5

Don't be surprised if this dinner disappears just as fast as it was prepared. Always use fresh basil when making this dish. It makes all the difference in the world. The marinara is ready when the noodles are, making this a very fast and easy meal to prepare on the fly. Don't forget the garlic bread!

extra virgin olive oil

3 garlic cloves, minced

½ cup fresh basil, chopped

1 tsp. red pepper flakes

1 can (28-oz.) peeled plum tomatoes

salt and fresh cracked black pepper, to taste

1 box (1-lb.) angel hair pasta

shredded Parmesan cheese

Drizzle extra virgin olive oil in a large saucepan on medium-high heat. Add garlic, basil, and red pepper flakes, and sauté for 1 minute. Be careful not to brown garlic. Add entire can of tomatoes with juice and crush with a spoon. Add salt and fresh cracked black pepper. Cover and simmer on low while cooking noodles.

Cook angel hair pasta according to package directions. Drain pasta and add to saucepan. Toss with tongs until pasta is fully coated with marinara. Serve with shredded Parmesan cheese.

FOGLIO SUNDAY SAUCE

SERVES 8-12

My Sunday sauce is the reason I wanted to write a dinner cookbook. The original recipe came from my Italian Grandma Foglio, and I have been making it for my own family for sixteen years, only tweaking it a tad. My Grandma Foglio used to make her own pasta in the morning and hung it all over her kitchen to dry. The sauce simmered all day, permeating the entire house. She used the tomato cans to add water to the sauce as it thickened and said it was ready when the grease around the top of the pot turned dark.

MEATBALLS

1 lb. ground beef

¼ cup fresh basil, chopped

2 garlic cloves, chopped

1 egg

¼ cup bread crumbs

¼ cup shredded Parmesan cheese

½ tsp. salt

½ tsp. fresh cracked black pepper

2 Tbsp. extra virgin olive oil

SAUCE

1 lb. beef stew meat or chuck roast, cubed

5–6 spicy Italian sausage links

1 (29-oz.) can whole peeled tomatoes in juice

3 (29-oz.) cans tomato sauce

1 (29-oz.) can tomato puree

1 cup fresh basil, chopped

2 garlic cloves, minced

¼ cup fresh parsley, chopped

1 Tbsp. Italian seasoning

salt and fresh cracked black pepper, to taste

1 (1-lb.) box spaghetti noodles

fresh basil, chopped, and shredded Parmesan cheese for topping

In a large bowl, make meatballs by adding the first 8 ingredients and mixing well. Roll meatballs into the size of a golf ball. Drizzle extra virgin olive oil in a large skillet and brown meat on all sides. Remove from pan and set aside.

Brown beef stew meat until browned on all sides and slightly pink in the center, 4–5 minutes. Remove from pan. Brown sausages on all sides 8 minutes, flipping over often. Remove from pan.

In a large stockpot, add all browned meat and remaining ingredients except noodles, basil, and Parmesan cheese. Cover and simmer for 3–4 hours on low heat, stirring often. Sauce will be thick. Add water a cup at a time to desired thickness. Add salt and fresh cracked black pepper to taste and more seasoning if desired.

Cook spaghetti noodles according to package directions. Drain in colander but do not rinse with water. Instead, drizzle with just a touch of extra virgin olive oil and toss with tongs before serving with sauce. Top spaghetti with fresh chopped basil and shredded Parmesan cheese.

CREAMY VODKA PENNE

SERVES 4-6

A rich and creamy Parmesan tomato sauce spiked with just a hint of vodka. Use the best vodka you can afford for superior taste in this delicious, easy-to-make dinner. If you are not a fan of penne, use any noodle you prefer.

1 (1-lb.) box penne pasta

3 Tbsp. extra virgin olive oil

1 tsp. crushed red pepper flakes

1 tsp. dried oregano

9 cloves garlic, thinly sliced lengthwise

1 (32-oz.) can whole peeled tomatoes in juice

¼ cup good-quality vodka

1 cup heavy cream

1 cup shredded Parmesan cheese

salt and fresh cracked black pepper, to taste

fresh basil and grated Parmesan cheese for garnish

Cook penne al dente in salted water according to package directions. Drain pasta and set aside.

In a saucepan, heat olive oil over medium heat and add red pepper flakes, oregano, and garlic, stirring until soft, 2 minutes. Add tomatoes and crush with spoon until small chunks remain. Add vodka and stir. Cook until reduced, 4 minutes.

Stir in cream and cheese, and add salt and fresh cracked black pepper to taste, and stir. Transfer cooked pasta to pot with sauce and toss until evenly coated. Sprinkle with basil and grated Parmesan cheese before serving.

EASY FRIED FISH

SERVES 6

Fish fry Sundays are a great escape from the typical casserole or Sunday sauce I often prepare. I like to serve my easy fried fish with Creamy Apple Coleslaw (page 111) and Sweet Hush Puppies (page 114). I like to enjoy this dinner on my deck with my family on a warm Summer evening and then wash it down with a tall glass of sweetened iced tea with lemon.

1 cup flour

1 tsp. salt

1 tsp. fresh cracked black pepper

½ tsp. paprika

2 cups canola oil

6–8 frozen whiting or tilapia fillets, thawed

Using a plate, lightly toss dry ingredients together until combined. Dredge each fillet in flour mixture on both sides ensuring full coverage. In a medium skillet, add canola oil (should be about 2 inches) and turn heat up to medium-high. Add fillets and cook until lightly golden brown, about 3 minutes. Flip and continue cooking for an additional 3 minutes until golden brown and fish begins to flake when tested with a fork. Remove with tongs or spatula onto a plate lined with paper towels for draining the oil. Do not stack fish on top of each other while draining. Additionally, you can place a cookie rack on the counter and place paper towels underneath. Lay the fish individually on cookie rack to drain. Serve hot.

ZESTY SHRIMP TACOS *with* FRESH MINT PINEAPPLE SALSA

SERVES 4-6

A spicy citrus marinade gives great flavor to shrimp in this delicious shrimp taco recipe. It's topped with a homemade sweet and spicy pineapple salsa dressed with fresh mint. Layers upon layers of flavor makes this dish incredibly enticing. You might want to double this recipe!

---

1 lb. frozen large shrimp, thawed and shells removed

MARINADE FOR SHRIMP

¼ cup lime juice

3 garlic cloves, minced

2 Tbsp. Worcestershire sauce

2 tsp. Old Bay® seasoning

salt and fresh cracked black pepper, to taste

SALSA

2 cups fresh pineapple, cut into small chunks

1 cup cilantro, chopped

1 jalapeño, diced

½ red onion, diced

2 Tbsp. lime juice

¼ tsp. salt

¼ tsp. cumin

fresh cracked black pepper, to taste

¼ cup fresh mint, chopped

TOPPING

cilantro

2 cups shredded pepper jack cheese

MARINADE

In a small bowl, prepare marinade by combining all ingredients. Place shrimp in a large freezer bag and add marinade. Seal bag and marinate for at least 1 hour. The longer you marinate, the stronger the flavor. While shrimp is marinating, prepare pineapple salsa.

In a large saucepan on medium heat, sauté shrimp with marinade until shrimp are pink and no longer opaque. Using tongs, place hot shrimp in taco shell and top with pineapple salsa, extra cilantro, and shredded pepper jack cheese.

SALSA

In a medium bowl, combine all salsa ingredients and cover. Let sit for at least 30 minutes, or longer for stronger flavor.

SLOW COOKER BEEF BOLOGNESE *over* FETTUCCINE

SERVES 4-6

This hearty bolognese sauce is full of fresh chopped vegetables and beefy flavor. It simmers all day in the slow cooker, melding the flavors together beautifully and making it a tasty and satisfying pasta dish to enjoy with your family. Serve with Italian bread and a salad to round out your meal.

1 lb. ground beef

1½ cups onion, finely chopped

½ cup carrots, finely chopped

½ cup celery, finely chopped

1 large garlic clove, minced

¾ cup chicken broth

½ cup dry red wine such as Pinot Noir

1 (14.5-oz.) can unsalted diced tomatoes, undrained

1 (28-oz.) can tomato sauce

½ tsp. dried parsley

1 tsp. dried Italian seasoning

½ tsp. fresh cracked black pepper

¼ tsp. salt

1 box fettuccine, cooked

In a large saucepan, cook ground beef until no longer pink on medium-high heat. Drain in colander and add to 4–6 quart slow cooker. In same pan, sauté the onion, carrot, celery, and garlic until fragrant and vegetables are tender, 5 minutes. Add to slow cooker. Add remaining ingredients and stir until well combined. Cook on medium high for 4–6 hours. Serve with cooked fettuccine or your favorite pasta.

QUICK SPINACH LASAGNA ROLLS

SERVES 4–6

When you are looking for a showstopping dinner to throw together in a hurry, this is it. Not only does this dish look amazing, but it's also a delicious recipe you can whip up and serve in less than an hour. The time saver is using jarred spaghetti sauce but feel free to use Foglio Sunday Sauce (page 33) for an extra special treat.

---

6 lasagna noodles

1 (10-oz.) package frozen chopped spinach, thawed and drained well

1 (15-oz.) container ricotta cheese

1 cup grated Parmesan cheese

1 egg

1 garlic clove, minced

1 tsp. dried Italian seasonings

½ cup fresh basil, finely chopped

salt and fresh cracked black pepper, to taste

1 (32-oz.) jar spaghetti sauce (any flavor and brand)

2 cups shredded mozzarella cheese

Preheat oven to 350 degrees. Cook lasagna noodles al dente according to package directions and lay flat on a clean lint-free towel to dry. Combine spinach, ricotta cheese, Parmesan cheese, egg, garlic, Italian seasonings, basil, salt, and fresh cracked black pepper in a medium bowl until combined.

Pour 1 cup of prepared spaghetti sauce on the bottom of a 9 × 13 baking dish.

Take ½ cup of ricotta/spinach mixture and spread evenly down the middle of each noodle. Sprinkle with a small amount (2 tablespoons) mozzarella cheese. Starting at on end, roll noodle carefully, making sure cheese filling doesn't seep out of the edges. Place seam side down in prepared baking dish. Repeat with remaining noodles.

Pour remaining sauce evenly over stuffed noodles and top each one with remaining mozzarella cheese.

Cover with aluminum foil and bake for 40 minutes until hot and bubbly and cheese is melted.

JALAPEÑO POPPER MAC AND CHEESE

SERVES 6-8

This embellished macaroni and cheese was inspired by my Dad's favorite jalapeño poppers recipe. It's made with all of the same ingredients—only it's tossed with macaroni and devoured by the forkful instead of by the handful.

---

1 lb. elbow macaroni

1 stick butter

1 cup Panko bread crumbs

2 cups half-and-half

1 (8-oz.) block of cream cheese, room temperature

2 cups shredded white cheddar cheese

1 cup shredded pepper jack cheese

2 jalapeños, 1 finely chopped and 1 thinly sliced

1 tsp. cayenne pepper

pinch of salt (if desired)

Set an oven rack 6 inches from the heat source and preheat the oven to 400 degrees.

Bring a large pot of salted water to a boil. Add the macaroni and cook al dente, 6 minutes. Drain pasta in a colander and set aside.

Melt butter in a microwavable bowl for 30 seconds or until melted. Mix with one cup of Panko crumbs and set aside.

In a large saucepan, heat half-and-half on medium heat until it comes to a simmer. Add the cream cheese and stir until completely melted. Whisk in the white cheddar and pepper jack cheeses until melted and the sauce is smooth and lump free. Stir in chopped jalapeño and pinch of salt. Add cooked pasta and mix thoroughly.

Pour pasta mixture into a 13 × 9 inch baking dish. Evenly spread Panko and butter mixture over macaroni and cheese. Lay the sliced jalapeños evenly on top of the bread crumbs and sprinkle with cayenne pepper. Bake until the cheese is bubbly and the bread crumbs are lightly browned and crispy, about 10 minutes.

CHEESY SPINACH TORTELLINI BAKE

SERVES 4-6

Jazz up ready-made cheese tortellini with a creamy garlic cheese sauce, mushrooms, onions, and spinach for an easy meal that's ready in less than 30 minutes. Bon appetito!

---

1 (19-oz.) package frozen cheese tortellini

1 (8-oz.) package fresh mushrooms, sliced

1 tsp. garlic salt

1 cup onion, diced

fresh cracked black pepper, to taste

½ cup butter, divided

1 garlic clove, minced

1 (12-oz.) can evaporated milk

2 cups shredded cheddar cheese

2 (10-oz.) packages frozen chopped spinach, thawed and squeezed dry

Preheat oven to 350 degrees. Cook tortellini according to package directions.

Meanwhile, in a large skillet, sauté mushrooms, garlic salt, onions, and fresh cracked black pepper in ¼ cup butter until mushrooms are tender. Add minced garlic clove and cook an additional minute until the garlic is fragrant but not golden. Remove from pan.

In same skillet, combine milk and remaining butter. Bring to a gentle boil. Stir in cheddar cheese until smooth. Add cooked tortellini and combine evenly. Stir in mushroom mixture and spinach, and gently combine.

Spread evenly to a greased 9 × 13 baking dish. Sprinkle with any remaining cheddar cheese if desired. Bake 20 minutes or until heated through and bubbly.

CREAMY VELVEETA CHEESEBURGER CASSEROLE

SERVES 6-8

An easy-to-prepare casserole that smells just like grilled cheeseburgers. The creamy Velveeta cheese sauce is tossed with spiral pasta and seasoned ground beef and then topped with all the classic burger fixings, baked until golden and bubbly. A kid-friendly favorite!

---

1 lb. uncooked rotini pasta

1 (16-oz.) block Velveeta cheese

1 cup half-and-half or whole milk

2 Tbsp. extra virgin olive oil

½ cup onion, diced

1 garlic clove, minced

1 lb. ground beef

1 tsp. all seasoning salt

½ tsp. fresh cracked black pepper

2 cups shredded cheddar cheese

3 dill pickles, chopped

shredded lettuce

8 slices tomato

ketchup and mustard for drizzling

Preheat oven to 350 degrees. Spray a 9 × 13 baking dish with cooking spray.

In a large pot, boil the pasta in salted water according to package directions until al dente. Drain pasta and set aside.

In a large saucepan on medium low heat, melt Velveeta cheese and half-and-half or milk. Mix until lump free and smooth. Remove from heat and set aside.

In a large skillet on medium-high heat, add olive oil and sauté onions until translucent. Using a garlic press, mince the garlic and sauté with the onions for 30 seconds.

Add the ground beef and seasoning salt and cook until no longer pink. Drain fat and return to the stove.

Add the drained noodles to the meat and stir well. Pour melted Velveeta cheese over beef and noodle mixture and mix until combined. Pour into the prepared baking pan and sprinkle with shredded cheddar cheese, dill pickles, lettuce, and tomato slices. Drizzle with ketchup and mustard, making squiggly lines or zigzags.

Bake in the oven for approximately 15 minutes or until cheese has melted and casserole is lightly golden and bubbly.

SHRIMP *and* ANDOUILLE SAUSAGE JAMBALAYA

SERVES 4-6

There is nothing quite like andouille sausage. The smokey Louisiana favorite makes this dish extremely flavorful and authentic to creole cooking. If you don't like heat, omit the red pepper flakes. To save time, be sure to purchase shrimp that is already shelled and deveined.

2 Tbsp. extra virgin olive oil

12 oz. andouille sausage

½ cup yellow onion, diced

1 cup green bell pepper, diced

1 cup celery, diced

4 cloves garlic, minced

1½ cups long grain rice

2 tsp. dried Italian seasoning

3 Tbsp. fresh basil, sliced in strips or torn to small pieces

⅛ tsp. ground cloves

1 tsp. chili powder

3 bay leaves

1 tsp. crushed red pepper flakes

salt and fresh cracked black pepper, to taste

1 (14-oz.) can chicken broth

1 (28-oz.) can whole tomatoes, chopped

1 pound frozen shrimp, peeled, deveined and thawed

Heat oil in a large stockpot over medium heat until hot. Add the andouille sausage, onion, green bell pepper, and celery. Cook for 2 minutes, stirring constantly. Add garlic and stir 1 minute more.

Add rice, Italian seasoning, basil, cloves, chili powder, bay leaves, red pepper flakes, and salt and fresh cracked black pepper, and stir.

Add the chicken broth and canned tomatoes (juice included). Using a spoon, press the tomatoes to crush. Bring to a boil.

Turn heat to low. Cook covered for 15 minutes. Add shrimp and stir. Cook for 5 more minutes uncovered until the rice is fluffy and all the shrimp is pink. Serve warm.

CHICKEN *and* BASIL STUFFED SHELLS *with* SAUCE

SERVES 6-8

The stuffed shells are packed with shredded chicken, fresh chopped basil, and cheeses, topped with prepared pasta sauce and baked until the cheese on top bubbles to perfection. Simple, delicious, and ready in less than an hour.

---

1 (16-oz.) package large pasta shells

1 (15-oz.) container whole milk ricotta cheese

1 garlic clove, minced

1 egg, slightly beaten

2 cups shredded Parmesan cheese, divided

2 cups shredded mozzarella cheese, divided

2 cups chicken breast, cooked and shredded

½ tsp. salt

½ tsp. fresh cracked black pepper

1 cup fresh basil, chopped

1 (26-oz.) jar pasta sauce (I use Prego® traditional)

1 tsp. Italian seasoning

Heat oven to 350 degrees. Cook and drain pasta according to package directions. Set aside.

In a medium bowl, mix ricotta cheese, garlic, egg, 1 cup Parmesan, 1 cup mozzarella, shredded chicken, salt, fresh cracked black pepper, and basil until well combined.

In a 9 × 13 casserole dish, spread ½ cup of sauce on the bottom. Spoon two tablespoons ricotta and chicken mixture into each shell. Place seem side up on sauce in baking dish. Pour remaining sauce over stuffed shells and sprinkle Italian seasoning. Top with remaining cheeses.

Cover with foil and bake for 35 minutes or until bubbly and cheese is slightly golden brown. Serve hot with Italian bread.

HOMESTYLE FAVORITE BEEF DINNERS

*Simple beefy main entrées full of big flavor
and perfect for hearty family dinners*

FIRECRACKER BARBACOA

SERVES 4-6

This slow-cooked shredded beef is so tender, juicy, and flavorful. It doesn't need anything more than flatbread to enjoy it with. But to make it extra special, I like to squeeze fresh lime juice on the beef and top with sour cream, cilantro, and salsa.

3 lbs. chuck roast, fat trimmed

3 cloves garlic, minced

3 chipotles from a (7-oz.) can of chipotles in adobo sauce

1 small white onion, finely chopped

⅓ cup fresh lime juice

2 Tbsp. apple cider vinegar

2 bay leaves

1 Tbsp. ground cumin

1 Tbsp. dried Italian seasoning

2 tsp. salt

1 tsp. fresh cracked black pepper

¼ tsp. ground cloves

1 cup beef stock

6–8 pieces Greek-style flatbread

TOPPINGS: lime, cilantro, sour cream, and salsa

Place roast into slow cooker. Combine remaining ingredients (not including the flatbread and toppings) in a separate bowl and stir to combine. Pour over roast and cover. Cook on low for 6–8 hours or on high for 3–4 hours, or until the beef is tender and falls apart easily when shredded with a fork.

Once beef is shredded, toss with its juices and let it sit 10 minutes. Use a pair of tongs or a slotted spoon to serve the barbacoa on Greek-style flatbread. Top it off with lime, cilantro, sour cream, and salsa if desired.

SLOW COOKER BALSAMIC THYME POT ROAST

SERVES 4-6

What I love about slow cookers is that they're self-basting for large pieces of meat like this wonderful pot roast. It cooks all day in a red wine balsamic beef broth with seasonings that bring out the flavor of the roast. By the time it's done cooking, the beef is so tender it cuts like butter.

---

1 (3–4 lb.) boneless beef chuck roast

1 tsp. salt

1 tsp. fresh cracked black pepper

2 Tbsp. extra virgin olive oil

1½ cups baby carrots

1 yellow onion, sliced

9 small red potatoes, cleaned and cut in half

½ cup dry red wine

2 cups beef stock

½ cup balsamic vinegar

2 Tbsp. brown sugar

1 tsp. chili paste

5–6 fresh thyme sprigs

Sprinkle roast with salt and fresh cracked black pepper. In a Dutch oven, heat oil over medium heat. Sear roast by browning on all sides in Dutch oven, about 1 minute per side. Remove from pan.

Add carrots, onions, and potatoes to the bottom of a slow cooker. Place seared pot roast on top of vegetables.

In a medium bowl, mix wine, beef stock, balsamic vinegar, brown sugar, and chili paste. Pour over meat in slow cooker and top with thyme sprigs.

Cover and cook on low for 6–8 hours or until roast is tender and edges can be shredded easily with a fork. Slice and serve with vegetables and remaining broth.

BEEF GRAVY SHEPHERD'S PIE

SERVES 6-8

Using brown gravy mix is a time saver in this classic shepherds pie recipe. It has rich beefy flavor with a little kick from the paprika sprinkled on top of the buttery, golden baked mashed potatoes. It's a fully loaded, all-in-one casserole that my family loves.

---

6 Yukon gold potatoes, peeled and cut in half

1 stick butter

⅓ cup sour cream

1 cup half-and-half

salt and fresh cracked black pepper, to taste

2 lbs. ground beef

½ of a yellow onion, diced

1 packet brown gravy mix

1 cup beef stock

2 Tbsp. Worcestershire sauce

1 (16-oz.) bag frozen peas and carrots, thawed

1 tsp. paprika

1 Tbsp. parsley flakes

Preheat oven to 375 degrees.

In a large stockpot, add peeled potatoes to boiling salted water. Cook 12 minutes or until potatoes are tender. Drain potatoes and put back into pot. Add butter, sour cream, half-and-half, salt, and fresh cracked black pepper. Mash with potato masher and stir mixture until smooth and thoroughly mixed. You should still have some lumps. Add additional half-and-half if mashed potatoes are too thick.

In a large skillet over medium-high heat, add beef and onions. Sauté until meat is no longer pink. Season with salt and fresh cracked black pepper to taste. Drain and return to pan. Add gravy mix, beef stock, and Worcestershire sauce. Stir until combined and mixture is boiling, 3 minutes. Add beef mixture to a 2-quart baking dish. Add peas and carrots over beef. Spread mashed potatoes evenly with back of spoon over beef. Sprinkle with paprika and parsley flakes.

Bake uncovered for 30 minutes or until mixture is bubbly and top is firm and light golden brown. Serve hot.

INDIVIDUAL GUINNESS BEEF POT PIES

SERVES 4

This rich stout beef stew is topped with a flaky puff pastry crust and perfectly portioned in individual ramekins. Don't let the small serving mislead you. This hearty, satisfying stew is full of chunky vegetables, potatoes, and tender beef. Round out this meal with buttermilk biscuits and a nice big salad.

2 lbs. beef chuck, cut into ½-inch cubes or cubed beef stew meat

salt and fresh cracked black pepper, to taste

2–3 Tbsp. extra virgin olive oil

½ cup yellow onion, diced

3 cloves garlic, minced

2 Tbsp. tomato paste

3 Tbsp. Worcestershire sauce

1 tsp. dried thyme

1 tsp. dried Italian seasoning

3 bay leaves

3 Tbsp. brown sugar

1½ cups Guinness stout

2 cups canned beef stock + 3 Tbsp. beef stock (to make paste)

2 Tbsp. flour, dissolved

2 cups diced potatoes

1 cup sliced carrots

1 cup frozen peas

1 (1-lb.) box puff pastry

1 egg, beaten with 1 Tbsp. water

Generously season beef pieces with salt and fresh cracked black pepper. Add olive oil to a hot Dutch oven or large pot. Brown the beef pieces on all sides in small batches. When browned, remove with a slotted spoon and set aside on plate.

Add diced onions to the same pot and sauté for 2–3 minutes until they are translucent. Add garlic and cook for 1 minute. Next, add the tomato paste, Worcestershire sauce, thyme, Italian seasoning, bay leaves, and brown sugar. Stir until incorporated. Add the beef back into the pot along with the juices.

Pour in the Guinness stout and beef stock. Turn heat up to medium-high heat, and bring the stew to a boil, about 5 minutes.

In a small bowl, combine flour and 3 tablespoons beef stock and mix until smooth. Add to boiling stew and stir well. Add potatoes and carrots. Turn the heat down, cover and simmer on low for an hour, stirring often. Add peas the last 15 minutes of cooking. Add salt and fresh cracked black pepper to taste.

Preheat oven to 400 degrees. Roll out puff pastry on a clean counter top to remove creases. Using standard ramekins (or any individual baking dishes you have on hand), place face down onto puff pastry and gently cut around dish using a sharp knife.

Ladle each ramekin with prepared stew and top with cut puff pastry. Stretch and press the pastry gently around the edges of the ramekin to prevent shrinkage while cooking.

In a small bowl lightly beat egg white and water. Brush puff pastry with egg mixture using a pastry brush. Using a knife, cut a slit in the middle of each pot pie.

Place prepared ramekins on a cookie sheet and bake in 400 degree oven for 20-25 minutes or until puff pastry is lightly golden brown and beef mixture is bubbly. Let sit for 10 minutes before serving.

LAYERED MEXICAN CASSEROLE

SERVES 6-8

This casserole is easy to make and packed with authentic Mexican flavors, layered with seasoned beef, flour tortillas, and traditional Mexican ingredients. A super hearty and flavorful meal that is filling and tastes superb with Fresh Hot Salsa (page 120).

6 (9-inch) round flour tortillas

⅔ lbs. ground beef

1 small yellow onion, diced

1 (16-oz.) can refried beans

3 Tbsp. taco seasoning

1 cup water

2 chipotle peppers in adobo sauce, sliced (from 7-oz. can)

1 (15-oz.) jar medium hot salsa (any brand)

1 cup black olives, sliced and divided

2 cups shredded cheddar cheese, divided

1 cup chopped green onions, divided

fresh cilantro

Preheat oven to 375 degrees. In a large saucepan, brown ground beef and onions until beef is no longer pink. Drain and return to pan. On medium heat, add refried beans and taco seasoning, stirring and breaking up refried beans with spoon, until heated and mixed thoroughly. Stir in water. Continue stirring until mixture is boiling and combined. Add 2 chipotle peppers with juice into meat mixture. Stir.

In a 3-quart baking dish sprayed with cooking spray, add 1 cup of salsa to the dish and spread across the bottom with back of spoon.

To assemble casserole, place two flour tortillas at bottom of baking dish, slightly overlapping. Add 2 cups meat mixture on top of tortillas, and spread evenly. Sprinkle with half of black olives, cheddar cheese, green onions, and cilantro. Top with two more flour tortillas and repeat. Top with remaining salsa, cheese, cilantro, and any remaining black olives and green onions.

Bake for 30 minutes uncovered until heated through and cheese is melted.

ITALIAN SAUSAGE *and* PEPPER HOAGIES

SERVES 6-8

Italian sausages are so flavorful that they make any meal delicious. Cook on the stove or grill and stuff them in a hoagie roll. Top with onion and peppers sautéed in garlic and spices, and you have yourself a simple meal packed with big flavor. I like to serve this BBQ-style with a side of Mom's Sweet Sausage Baked Beans (page 118).

¼ cup extra virgin olive oil

1 lb. sweet or spicy Italian sausage

2 red peppers, sliced

2 green bell peppers, sliced

2 yellow onions, sliced

1 tsp. kosher salt

1 tsp. fresh cracked black pepper

1 tsp. dried oregano

1 tsp. dried basil leaves

3 garlic cloves, chopped

4–6 fresh Italian sandwich rolls, optional

Heat the oil in a heavy large skillet over medium heat. Add the sausages and cook until brown on both sides, 7–10 minutes. Remove from pan and drain.

Using the same pan over medium heat, add peppers, onions, salt, and fresh cracked black pepper, and cook until soft and tender and slightly golden brown on the edges, 5 minutes. Add the oregano, basil, and garlic, and cook 3 more minutes, tossing to combine. Serve sausages on hoagie rolls and top with onions and peppers.

TO GRILL SAUSAGES

Sear the sausages by placing on the grill over moderate direct heat to brown the skin. Turn the links frequently using tongs. Brown all sides to a golden or deep brown; avoid blackening or burning the skins.

Move the sausage links to an area of the grill where they receive indirect heat and close the cover on the grill. Cook the sausage slowly until internal temperatures reach 160 degrees.

SPICY BEEF SWEET POTATO STIR-FRY

SERVES 4-6

This stir-fry dinner is simple to prepare and full of exciting flavors. The sweet potatoes in this spicy meal make it a sweet/heat recipe that I love. It's a tasty party-in-your-mouth kind of meal that's colorful and amazing in taste, texture, and appeal.

4 Tbsp. sesame oil, divided

1 sweet potato, cut into strips

3 red chili peppers

1 yellow onion, sliced

2 garlic cloves, minced

2 Tbsp. fresh ginger, peeled and finely chopped

1 lb. flank steak

salt and fresh cracked black pepper, to taste

4 green onions, cut into 2-inch strips

½ cup water

½ cup soy sauce, plus more for serving

3 Tbsp. sugar

1 tsp. chili paste

fresh cilantro leaves for garnish

cooked white rice for serving

In a large, heavy frying pan or wok, add 2 tablespoons sesame oil on high heat. Add sweet potato, chilies, and onion, and stir-fry until potatoes are tender, 2 minutes. Add garlic and ginger and stir until fragrant and heated through, or about 1 minute. Remove from pan onto a plate and set aside.

Cut the steak in half lengthwise. Cut the halves against the grain into slices ⅛-inch thick.

In same pan, heat another 2 tablespoons of oil and sear the beef for 1 minute without stirring. Then stir-fry the beef until the meat is no longer pink. Add salt and fresh cracked black pepper to taste. Add vegetable mixture to the beef and heat through. Toss in sliced green onions.

In a medium bowl, mix together water, soy sauce, sugar, and chili paste. Pour over beef and vegetable mixture, stirring until mixture is heated through and thickened. Serve over rice and garnish with cilantro and extra soy sauce if desired.

PHILLY CHEESESTEAK PIZZA

SERVES 4

This pizza is a hit with Philly Cheesesteak lovers. The lightly seasoned flank steak is tender and juicy, and the cheese is melted and marvelous. For a time saver, use a pre-baked pizza crust when your Sundays are busy spending time with family. Double the recipe for a crowd, and be sure to have the recipe on hand—you'll be asked to make a copy!

---

3 Tbsp. extra virgin olive oil, divided

2 lbs. flank steak, cut into strips

salt and fresh cracked black pepper, to taste

1 green bell pepper, cut into strips

1 red onion, cut into strips

1 Tbsp. oregano

1 garlic clove, minced

1 pre-baked (12-inch) round pizza crust

2 cups shredded provolone cheese or mozzarella, divided

1 tsp. paprika

In a large saucepan, add 2 tablespoons olive oil, steak strips, and salt and fresh cracked black pepper. Cook on medium-high heat until browned. Remove meat from pan and transfer to a cutting board. Add onions and green pepper to same pan, and sauté five minutes or until onion is translucent and peppers are soft. Add beef back to pan, and add oregano and garlic.

Brush pre-baked pizza crust with 1 tablespoon olive oil. Sprinkle one cup of cheese evenly on crust. Add beef, onion, and pepper mixture evenly. Add remaining cheese and sprinkle paprika over entire pizza.

Bake in a preheated oven at 375 degrees for 12 minutes or until cheese is bubbly and crust is lightly golden brown. Serve immediately.

BIG FLAVOR HOISIN BURGERS *with* DIJON HOISIN SAUCE

SERVES 6-8

Skip the ketchup and mustard for your next burger and try this amazing Asian-inspired patty that has the robust flavors of hoisin sauce, ginger, curry, and jalapeño. Once grilled, top this juicy burger with a homemade Dijon mustard hoisin sauce that's simple to prepare and worth the extra step. You'll never eat a burger the old way again. Simply delicious!

---

1 jalapeño, seeded and diced small

½ cup diced red bell pepper, plus more for garnish

1 tsp. curry powder

2 cloves of garlic, minced

2 Tbsp. ginger, finely minced

2 green onions, diced small, plus more for garnish

3 Tbsp. store-bought hoisin sauce

3 lbs. ground beef

salt and fresh cracked black pepper, to taste

lettuce for garnish

hamburger buns with sesame seeds

HOMEMADE DIJON
HOISIN SAUCE

¼ cup store-bought hoisin sauce

2 Tbsp. Dijon mustard

2 Tbsp. water

½ tsp. honey

salt and fresh cracked black pepper, to taste

In a large bowl combine first seven ingredients with ground beef until thoroughly combined.

Preheat a grill to medium high. Form the beef into 6-ounce patties, 1 inch thick. Season the patties on both sides with salt and fresh cracked black pepper.

Brush the grill grates with vegetable oil or spray with grill cooking spray. Grill the patties 5 minutes on one side. Flip patties and cook until marked on the bottom and slightly firm, 3 more minutes or until no longer pink.

During the last minute of grilling, brush the patties with the homemade Dijon hoisin sauce. Move the patties to a plate and let rest 5 minutes. Serve on bun with lettuce and homemade Dijon hoisin sauce for topping.

HOMEMADE DIJON HOISIN SAUCE
In a small bowl, combine all ingredients with a whisk until smooth.

HOMESTYLE CAJUN DIRTY RICE

SERVES 6-8

Authentic Cajun spices add pizazz to this tasty home-cooked Louisiana dirty rice. The secret ingredient that adds massive flavor is pureed chicken livers. Once cooked, the chicken livers look just like ground beef, so if you have picky eaters, they'll never know what they are eating but their taste buds will know that it's one amazing tasty dirty rice dish.

---

2 cups chicken broth

1 cup long-grain white rice

2 Tbsp. butter

1 lb. lean ground beef

¼ cup chicken livers, puréed in food processor

1 cup onions, finely chopped

3 celery stalks, finely chopped

1 red bell pepper, seeded and finely chopped

3 garlic cloves, minced

½ tsp. cayenne pepper

1 tsp. cajun seasoning

1 tsp. oregano

1 tsp. parsley

3 green onions, thinly sliced

salt and fresh cracked black pepper, to taste

In a 1½-quart saucepan over high heat, bring the chicken broth to a boil. Stir in the rice and return to a boil. Reduce the heat to low, cover with lid, and cook for 20 minutes. Uncover and use a fork to check if the liquid is absorbed and the rice is soft. Re-cover and cook for a few more minutes if liquid remains. Remove from the heat and keep covered while you prepare the meat.

Melt butter in a large frying pan over medium heat. Add the ground beef, puréed chicken livers, onion, celery, red bell pepper, garlic, cayenne pepper, cajun seasoning, oregano, and parsley. Sauté for 3 minutes. Reduce the heat to medium-low and cook, stirring frequently, until the vegetables are tender and the flavors have come together, 20 minutes.

Add green onions to the meat mixture and cook, stirring frequently, 3 minutes. Add the cooked rice as well as the salt and fresh cracked black pepper, stirring frequently, until heated through and thoroughly combined.

CREAMY SLOW COOKER BEEF STROGANOFF

SERVES 6-8

A mushroom-flavored wine sauce is gently simmered in a slow cooker with tender beef and smothered over top of egg noodles. The best part of cooking with wine is the leftovers. Pour yourself a glass to go with your stroganoff and enjoy!

---

2 lbs. beef stew meat

2 Tbsp. extra virgin olive oil

salt and fresh cracked black pepper, to taste

2 Tbsp. butter

1 cup yellow onion, chopped

1 (8-oz.) package of sliced mushrooms

1 garlic clove, minced

1 Tbsp. Worcestershire sauce

1 (10.5-oz.) can cream of mushroom soup

½ cup chardonnay or dry white wine

¼ cup water

1 tsp. dried parsley

1 (12-oz.) package large egg noodles

4 (8-oz.) blocks cream cheese

In a large saucepan, sear beef in hot olive oil until browned evenly on all sides. Sprinkle with salt and fresh cracked black pepper to taste. Place in slow cooker.

In same pan, add butter on medium heat and sauté the mushrooms and onions just until tender, about 3 minutes. Toss with minced garlic and heat until just combined and garlic is fragrant, 1 minute. Add to slow cooker.

In a small bowl, stir the Worcestershire sauce, soup, wine, and water. Pour over beef in slow cooker. Add parsley. Cook on low for 6–8 hours.

In a large saucepan, heat salted water to a boil. Cook egg noodles according to package directions. Drain noodles and set aside.

Stir cream cheese into beef mixture until melted. Continue stirring on high heat until fully melted and mixture is thickened. If you want a creamier stroganoff, add entire block of cream cheese. Serve over cooked egg noodles.

PLANTAIN PICADILLO

SERVES 4-6

A flavorful beef and rice recipe that reminds me of my Puerto Rican grandmother. She used to make us ground beef and rice with raisins and the savory/sweet combo has always been my favorite. I added plantains in her honor since she always fried them up for us for snacking when we were with her. For a time saver, serve plantain picadillo with instant Mexican or white rice.

---

1 lb. ground beef

3 Tbsp. extra virgin olive oil, divided

1 ripe plantain, sliced and cut into fourths

½ onion, chopped

1 jalapeño, seeds removed and finely diced

1 green bell pepper, diced

3 garlic cloves, minced

½ cup white wine

½ cup raisins (can use golden raisins)

1 Tbsp. tomato paste

1 (14.5-oz.) can stewed tomatoes

1 Tbsp. adobo seasoning

2 tsp. dried oregano

salt and fresh cracked black pepper, to taste

In a large skillet, brown ground beef. Drain and set aside. In same skillet, heat 2 tablespoons oil in large skillet over medium-high heat. Add plantains and cook until lightly golden brown. Plantains will stick, so be sure to continuously stir them while cooking. Remove from pan.

Add another tablespoon oil and sauté onion, jalapeño, and green bell pepper until softened, about 5 minutes or until onion is translucent. Add garlic and stir 1 more minute until fragrant.

Add wine, raisins, tomato paste, stewed tomatoes, adobo seasoning, and oregano. Stir to combine until heated through, breaking up the stewed tomatoes with a spatula.

Add meat and stir. Cover and reduce heat to medium-low for 10 minutes. Add salt and fresh cracked black pepper to taste. Serve with Mexican rice or white rice.

SIMPLE SALISBURY STEAK *with* ONION MUSHROOM GRAVY *and* MASHED POTATOES

SERVES 4

A time-saving way to make a great classic dish is to use a jar of ready-made beef gravy and jazz it up with sautéed mushrooms and onions. In this recipe, the lightly seasoned salisbury steak is cooked then simmered in the gravy and poured over mashed potatoes.

MASHED POTATOES

2 tsp. salt, divided

3 lbs. russet potatoes, peeled and sliced in half

1 stick butter

1 cup whole milk

½ tsp. fresh cracked black pepper

SALISBURY STEAK

1 lb. ground beef

⅓ cup plain dry bread crumbs

2 garlic cloves, minced

2 Tbsp. Worcestershire sauce

2 tsp. Italian seasoning

1 egg, beaten

1 Tbsp. vegetable oil

ONION MUSHROOM GRAVY

1 Tbsp. butter

1 (8-oz.) container fresh mushrooms

1 large onion, sliced in rings

1 (18-oz.) jar beef gravy

Bring a large pot of water with 1 teaspoon of salt to a boil. Add potatoes and return to a boil. Boil until tender, about 15 to 20 minutes, and drain in a colander. Return potatoes to stockpot and add stick of butter. Using a potato masher, mash potatoes until a few medium chunks are left. Add milk and 1 teaspoon salt and fresh cracked black pepper. Continue mashing to desired consistency and mixture is completely combined. Cover and keep warm. Set aside.

Combine the beef, bread crumbs, garlic, Worcestershire sauce, Italian seasoning, and egg in a medium bowl. Shape into 4 (½-inch thick) oval patties.

Heat oil in a large skillet over medium-high heat. Add the patties and cook for 5 minutes. Then flip and cook another 5 minutes or until well browned on both sides. Remove patties and drain fat off pan.

Add butter to same pan. On medium heat, cook the mushrooms and onion for 3–5 minutes until soft and onions are translucent. Add gravy and stir. Bring mixture to a boil. Add beef back to pan and flip, covering the patty with gravy. Lower heat and simmer covered for 10 minutes. Remove from heat and serve over mashed potatoes.

MONGOLIAN BEEF

SERVES 4

SAUCE

6 Tbsp. soy sauce

½ Tbsp. sugar

2 tsp. cornstarch

2 Tbsp. hoisin sauce

1 Tbsp. chili paste

4 tsp. rice vinegar

4 Tbsp. orange juice

BEEF

1 Tbsp. sesame oil

1¼ lbs. flank steak, cut across the grain into thin strips

salt and pepper, to taste

2 garlic cloves, minced

1 Tbsp. ginger, minced

½ cup green scallions

1 (16-oz.) package wide lo mein noodles

sesame seeds for garnish

In a small bowl combine soy sauce, sugar, cornstarch, hoisin sauce, chili paste, rice vinegar and orange juice. Whisk until smooth and combined. Set aside.

In a stir-fry pan or large skillet, add sesame oil. On medium-high heat, stir-fry flank steak until no longer pink, about 2 minutes. Sprinkle lightly with salt and pepper, to taste.

Turn heat to medium-low heat and add garlic, ginger, and green scallions. Stir-fry another 2 minutes.

Pour the sauce mixture over the meat and cook until it has thickened, 2–3 minutes.

Cook lo mein noodles according to package directions. Serve beef over cooked noodles and sprinkle with sesame seeds.

WARM YOU UP
SOUPS AND STEWS

The comforts of home simmer on the stove on a lazy Sunday afternoon with sensational soups and stews. They're hearty enough all on their own or you can add a salad and baguette to round out your meal.

HOLIDAY LENTIL SOUP

SERVES 8-10

Years ago, my uncle made a simple lentil soup for Thanksgiving. One year I took over the soup detail and added turmeric and fresh basil and quadrupled the tomato sauce called for in my uncle's recipe. This new and improved version is a little more distinctive and full of fantastic flavor. My family likes to eat this sensational soup with a sprinkle of shredded Parmesan cheese on top to make it extra special.

---

1 lb. ground beef

salt and fresh cracked black pepper, to taste, for browning ground beef

1 (15.5-oz.) bag of lentils

1 (16-oz.) bag peeled mini carrots

10 cups water, divided

3 large russet potatoes, chopped

2 Tbsp. turmeric

1 Tbsp. Italian seasoning

2 (28-oz.) cans tomato sauce

1 tsp. salt

2 tsp. fresh cracked black pepper

1 cup fresh basil, chopped

shredded Parmesan cheese, for topping if desired

In a large saucepan, brown ground beef. Season with salt and fresh cracked black pepper and drain. Add to large stockpot. Rinse lentils in colander according to package directions. Add to stockpot.

In a blender, blend entire bag of carrots with 7 cups of water or just enough to cover carrots. Crush carrots to small bits. Pour entire contents of blender into stockpot with ground beef. Add remaining ingredients and bring to a boil. Simmer uncovered on medium low heat for 3–4 hours. Stir frequently.

As the lentils cook, the soup will begin to thicken. Add 3 more cups of water one cup at a time to thin it out to desired consistency as the soup cooks. Be careful not to add too much water as it will dilute the taste of the soup.

Adjust seasonings if necessary by adding more basil, Italian seasoning, or salt and fresh cracked black pepper to taste. Serve with Parmesan cheese sprinkled on top if desired.

CURRY PUMPKIN SOUP

SERVES 8-10

I have been making this incredibly creamy pumpkin curry soup on Halloween night for years. We like to warm our bellies before the chilly trick-or-treat night ensues. My neighbors still ask for samples each year when they bring their little goblins by for candy. It's so delicious, it's simply unforgettable.

½ cup pumpkin seeds (optional)

½ cup diced onion

¼ stick of butter

3 Tbsp. flour

1½ Tbsp. curry powder

1 (32-oz.) can vegetable broth

1 (29-oz.) can pureed pumpkin

2 cups half-and-half plus more for serving (optional)

3 Tbsp. soy sauce

¼ cup plus 1 Tbsp. sugar

¼ tsp. salt

¼ tsp. fresh cracked black pepper

Preheat oven to 375 degrees. Arrange pumpkin seeds in a single layer on a baking sheet. Toast in preheated oven for 10 minutes, or until seeds begin to brown.

Add onions to butter in a large stockpot over medium heat. Sauté for 1 minute. Whisk in flour and curry powder until smooth. Gradually whisk in broth, and cook until soup is thickened and flour mixture is almost dissolved.

Whisk in pumpkin and half-and-half. Season with soy sauce, sugar, salt, and fresh cracked black pepper. Bring just to a boil, and then remove from heat. Garnish with roasted pumpkin seeds.

DAD'S CHICKEN NOODLE SOUP

SERVES 8-10

The best memories of growing up were Sunday dinners that my Dad frequently prepared. His recipes always simmered all day long, getting more and more delicious as the minutes went by. I asked him to hand over his chicken noodle soup recipe for this book because it's one of his best recipes and my all-time childhood favorite dinner.

---

4 cups homemade chicken stock, or 4 large chicken bouillon cubes

1 (4–lb.) whole chicken

3 medium potatoes, diced

1 cup carrots, peeled and sliced

½ cup white onion, diced

2 Tbsp. salt

1 Tbsp. fresh cracked black pepper

¼ cup fresh parsley, chopped

6 oz. of light and fluffy medium egg noodles (half 12-oz. bag)

To make chicken stock, first rinse chicken in cold water and remove chicken giblets. Set aside. Place chicken in a large 6-quart stockpot and fill with water, just covering chicken. Boil for one hour. Carefully remove chicken with large tongs or two large service spoons and place in a large colander, reserving broth. Skim fat off the top with a large spoon. Rinse chicken in cold water. Discard chicken skin.

Pick meat off bones and shred with fingers, removing any fat that may be visible. Add shredded chicken back to chicken stock. Add chicken giblets and a few chicken bones for flavoring broth.

Add vegetables to pot. Add a cup more of water if needed. Add salt, fresh cracked black pepper, and parsley. Continue to add more to taste if needed. Turn heat to low and simmer for two hours. Remove bones, and add noodles to pot, keeping the heat to low. Cook for 7–8 minutes or until noodles are tender. Serve immediately after.

PASTA *e* FAGIOLI

SERVES 8-10

I love that this soup is full of great Italian flavor, pasta, and vegetables. It's perfect for a winter's day to warm you up and savor by the fireplace. Using spicy sausage instead of ground beef gives it distinct flavor with just a hint of spiciness. If you are not a fan of spice, simply swap out the spicy sausage for sweet. It is sure to taste just as fabulous.

1 cup bow-tie pasta

2 Tbsp. extra virgin olive oil, divided

1 lb. spicy Italian sausage links, casing removed

3 cloves garlic, minced

1 onion, diced

3 carrots, peeled and diced

3 stalks celery, diced

1 (15-oz.) can chicken stock

1 (16-oz.) can tomato sauce

1 (28-oz.) can crushed tomatoes

1 (8-oz.) can Italian seasoned stewed tomatoes

1 Tbsp. dried basil

1½ tsp. dried oregano

½ tsp. dried thyme

½ cup water

1 (15-oz.) can dark red kidney beans, drained and rinsed

1 (15-oz.) can great northern beans, drained and rinsed

salt and fresh cracked black pepper, to taste

Cook pasta according to package directions in a large pot of salted water; drain well and set aside.

Heat 1 tablespoon extra virgin olive oil in a large Dutch oven over medium heat. Add Italian sausage to prepared skillet and cook until browned, 3–5 minutes. Crumble sausage while cooking. Drain excess fat and set aside.

Add remaining 1 tablespoon oil to Dutch oven. Stir in garlic, onion, carrots, and celery. Cook, stirring occasionally, until tender, 3–4 minutes.

Whisk in chicken stock, tomato sauce, crushed tomatoes, stewed tomatoes, basil, oregano, thyme, water, beans, and Italian sausage. Season with salt and fresh cracked black pepper, to taste. Bring to a boil and then reduce heat. Simmer covered until vegetables are tender, 10–15 minutes. Stir in pasta and beans, and simmer for 10 more minutes or until pasta is cooked al dente.

FRENCH ONION SOUP

SERVES 6

One year for Christmas I wanted to make French onion soup for my family. I ordered stoneware French onion soup crocks and made a very flavorful soup that was a big hit. I love melted cheese so this recipe is one of my favorites.

4 Tbsp. butter

2 lbs. yellow onions, sliced

½ Tbsp. sugar

1 Tbsp. flour

1 cup dry white wine (chardonnay)

6 cups beef stock

3 beef bouillon cubes

1 tsp. dried thyme

2 bay leaves

salt and fresh cracked black pepper, to taste

1 baguette, sliced

6 slices mozzarella cheese

Melt butter in a large Dutch oven or heavy pot on medium-low heat. Add onions. Sprinkle with sugar and cook, until they are soft, golden brown, and beginning to caramelize, about 1 hour.

Sprinkle flour over onions, and stir to coat. Add wine, beef stock, bouillon, thyme, and bay leaves, and bring to a simmer. Cook, partially covered, for 30 minutes. Season with salt and fresh cracked black pepper to taste.

Turn oven to broiler setting. Ladle hot soup into six ovenproof bowls, leaving room at the top for a baguette. Arrange the bowls on a baking pan. Place 1 slice of bread in each bowl of soup. Add one or two slices of mozzarella cheese. Place under the broiler until cheese is melted and golden around the edges. Watch carefully that cheese doesn't burn. Serve immediately.

DINA'S ULTIMATE CINNAMON CHILI *with* BEANS

SERVES 8-10

Coffee, cinnamon, cocoa, and brown sugar are my secret ingredients in this unique and flavorful chili. The cinnamon adds a sweet heat that compliments the coffee and cocoa while all three bring out the flavor of the tomatoes. The rich, complex flavors are apparent in every hearty spoonful.

---

2 lbs. ground beef

2 (29-oz.) cans tomato sauce

1 (29-oz.) can crushed tomatoes

2 (15.5-oz.) cans red kidney beans, undrained

2 (15.5-oz.) cans black beans, undrained

1 can water (from 29-oz. can)

1 Tbsp. chili powder

1 tsp. cumin

1 tsp. Italian seasoning

1 tsp. paprika

1 tsp. cinnamon

3 Tbsp. brown sugar

½ tsp. cayenne pepper

½ cup strong brewed coffee

2 Tbsp. dark Dutch process cocoa powder (or regular unsweetened cocoa powder)

2–3 garlic cloves, minced

1 jalapeño, finely diced

salt and fresh cracked black pepper, to taste

1 cup or handful of fresh cilantro, chopped

TOPPINGS: sour cream, shredded cheese

In a large stockpot or Dutch oven, brown ground beef. Drain and return meat to pot. Add the rest of the ingredients except for the cilantro. Stir constantly until chili comes to a full boil. Then reduce heat and cook uncovered for 2 hours, stirring occasionally. Add cilantro and adjust seasonings to desired taste and cook another 5 minutes. Serve in bowls and top with additional fresh cilantro, a dollop of sour cream, and shredded cheddar cheese if desired.

SLOW COOKER BEEF BURGUNDY

SERVES 4-6

This recipe has all the comforts of home in the slow cooker. Tender beef and flavorful veggies with earthy seasonings slow cooked in a rich wine sauce make this bowl of goodness a meal that warms the heart. This stew is even better the next day, and it makes a great make-ahead meal.

6–7 pieces thick cut bacon, cooked

3 lbs. lean beef stew meat

1 tsp. salt

1 tsp. fresh cracked black pepper

4 Tbsp. flour

1 lb. fresh petite baby bella mushrooms

1 (14-oz.) bag frozen pearl onions, thawed

1 lb. baby carrots or sliced carrots

2 cups Pinot Noir or Burgundy

3 cups beef stock

2 Tbsp. tomato paste

2 cloves garlic, minced

3 bay leaf, crumbled

1 tsp. dried parsley

1 tsp. dried thyme

salt and fresh cracked black pepper, to taste

baguette, sliced

In a large saucepan, cook bacon until slightly crispy. Remove bacon from pan with slotted spoon or tongs, leaving drippings in pan. Set bacon aside.

In a large sealable plastic bag, add beef stew meat. Add salt and fresh cracked black pepper and shake to coat meat. Add flour and shake until all pieces are evenly coated. Heat saucepan to medium-high heat and sear meat in bacon drippings on all sides for 2 minutes. Center should still be left a little pink.

Turn slow cooker on medium high. Add beef, bacon, mushrooms, onions, and carrots. Pour in wine. Measure beef stock in a large glass measuring cup. Mix tomato paste and garlic in beef stock until combined. Pour over meat in slow cooker. Add bay leaf, parsley and thyme. Stir. Cook in slow cooker on low for 5–7 hours. When ready, turn off slow cooker and stir well. Add more salt and fresh cracked black pepper to taste and serve with sliced baguette.

THAI COCONUT SHRIMP SOUP

SERVES 4-6

The shrimp in this soup is an added bonus because the broth is so delicious that it takes center stage. The complex flavors are powerful together, yet the soup is fresh and light with just a hint of spiciness. If you like bread with your soup, buy a baguette, slice it up, and dip it into the delicious broth.

3–4 Tbsp. sesame oil, for cooking

4 garlic cloves, minced

1 Tbsp. minced fresh ginger

1 (8-oz.) container sliced mushrooms

1 red bell pepper, diced

1 lb. peeled and deveined large shrimp (30–40)

4 cups vegetable broth

1 (25.5-oz.) can unsweetened coconut milk

3 Tbsp. fish sauce

3 Tbsp. light brown sugar

2 Tbsp. lime juice

1 Tbsp. curry powder

2 tsp. chili paste

salt and fresh cracked black pepper, to taste

¼ cup cilantro

½ cup green onions, sliced thin

In a large stockpot, add sesame oil and sauté garlic, ginger, mushrooms, and red bell pepper on medium heat until tender, 2 minutes. Add shrimp and cook until pink on both sides. Add broth, coconut milk, fish sauce, brown sugar, lime juice, curry powder, and chili paste, stirring constantly until a light boil. Turn heat down and simmer for 5 minutes. Add salt and fresh cracked black pepper to taste. Stir in cilantro and green onion.

CREAMY CHICKEN TOMATO STEW

SERVES 8-10

---

4 Tbsp. extra virgin olive oil, divided

3 chicken breasts

salt and fresh cracked black pepper, to taste

1 green pepper, diced

1 yellow pepper, diced

½ cup red onion, finely chopped

3 celery stalks, finely chopped

1 jalapeño with seeds, diced

2 garlic cloves, minced

1 tsp. oregano

1 (48-oz.) can chicken broth

4 (14.5-oz.) cans stewed tomatoes

1 cup half-and-half

1 box ribbon pasta or mini rotini, cooked according to package directions

In a large saucepan, heat 2 tablespoons olive oil on medium high heat. On a clean countertop, pound three chicken breasts with a meat tenderizer and sprinkle each breast on both sides with salt and pepper to taste. Set chicken aside.

In a large Dutch oven, add 2 tablespoons olive oil and sauté green pepper, yellow pepper, red onion, celery, and jalapeño for 3 minutes or until fragrant and partially translucent, stirring constantly. Add garlic and stir for 1 minute. Add remaining ingredients except for half-and-half and pasta. Bring to a boil. Turn heat down to medium-low and cook for 1 hour. Add half-and-half and pasta (about 2 cups cooked or as much as you prefer) and salt and pepper to taste. Cook an additional 30 minutes on medium-low heat until stew is simmering and flavors are blended together.

WHITE BEAN CHICKEN HABAÑERO SOUP

SERVES 6-8

This soup has sriracha, which is a spicy blend of red chilies, vinegar, and garlic. It adds tangy heat to this white bean soup packed with shredded chicken, spices, cilantro, corn, and spicy habañero peppers. It's super delicious and satisfying and perfect to warm your tummy on a cold winter's night.

1–2 Tbsp. extra virgin olive oil

5 chicken breasts

2 (14.5-oz.) cans white beans, drain and rinsed

1 (15-oz.) can sweet corn, drained

1 Tbsp. oil

1 jalapeño pepper, minced

1 habañero pepper, chopped

1 large onion, chopped

4 garlic cloves, minced

salt and fresh cracked black pepper

1 Tbsp. ground cumin

1 tsp. sriracha

1 tsp. chili powder

8 cups chicken broth

1 cup fresh cilantro, chopped

shredded Mexican cheese blend (or shredded Monterrey jack), for topping

In a large Dutch oven, add extra virgin olive oil. Pound chicken with a meat tenderizer and salt and pepper both sides of chicken. Cook until no longer pink. Shred and place back in stockpot.

Add remaining ingredients except cilantro and cheese. Use a colander to drain and rinse beans before adding to stockpot. Bring soup to a boil. Then simmer on medium-low heat for 1 hour. Add chopped fresh cilantro and stir. Top with shredded cheese.

HADDOCK STEW

SERVES 4-6

If you are a fan of fish, you'll love it simmered with a white wine, tomato-based chicken broth, seasonings and vegetables. It's the perfect way to change up the way you eat your fresh caught or frozen fillets. This stew is a keeper for any fish lover.

---

1 (10-oz.) bag pearl onions

2 Tbsp. extra virgin olive oil

2 garlic cloves, chopped

1 jalapeño, chopped

4 celery stalks, chopped

2 tsp. dried parsley

2 (14.5-oz.) cans stewed tomatoes

2 Tbsp. tomato paste

1½ cups white wine (such as Sauvignon Blanc)

1 tsp. thyme

½ tsp. fennel

¼ tsp. sriracha

1 (49-oz.) can chicken stock, plus 1 chicken bouillon cube

2 lbs. white fish fillets (I used haddock) cut into bite-sized pieces

salt and fresh cracked black pepper, to taste

Prepare pearl onions according to package directions and set aside. In a large stockpot, add olive oil and sauté garlic, jalapeño, and celery, and cook for 3 minutes on medium heat.

Add remaining ingredients and cook, stirring often, for 1 hour on medium-low heat. Add salt and fresh cracked black pepper to taste. Sprinkle with extra parsley if desired before serving.

FRESH HOMEMADE SIDES

This cookbook will make it easier than ever to prepare a delicious side dish made with simple, fresh ingredients. Although these recipes are meant to be served on the side, they're so delectable that they often take center stage!

ROASTED ASPARAGUS *with* LEMON *and* PARMESAN

SERVES 4

A few simple ingredients turn ordinary asparagus into a superb, tasty side dish. Blanching the asparagus will make it tender and bright green, helping the dish to look as wonderful as it tastes.

1 bundle fresh asparagus

1 lemon

2 Tbsp. extra virgin olive oil

salt and fresh cracked black pepper, to taste

¼ cup shredded Parmesan cheese

Preheat oven to 400 degrees. Trim asparagus ends (the hard ends). Blanch the asparagus by immersing in a boiling pot of water for two minutes. Place asparagus in a colander, run it under very cold water, and drain.

Thinly slice half of a lemon. Spread asparagus on large cookie sheet and sprinkle with the other lemon half. Toss with olive oil. Sprinkle with salt and fresh cracked black pepper and Parmesan cheese. Top with lemon slices.

Place in oven and roast for 6–7 minutes. Using tongs, carefully turn asparagus over and sprinkle with more Parmesan cheese if desired. Continue roasting for another 8 minutes or until asparagus is tender and cheese is a slight golden brown on the edges.

GARLIC MASHED POTATOES

SERVES 4

---

6 medium russet potatoes, peeled and chopped

1 stick unsalted butter, room temperature

⅓ cup sour cream

1 garlic clove, minced

1 cup whole milk

salt and fresh cracked black pepper, to taste

In a medium saucepan, cook potatoes in salted water until tender, about 15 minutes. Drain the potatoes and return them to the saucepan.

Add butter and mash the potatoes with a potato masher or the back of a fork until potatoes are broken up and lightly mashed. Add remaining ingredients and continue mashing until fluffy and mixture is blended. Add more milk if a thinner consistency is desired. Salt and pepper to taste.

CREAMY APPLE COLESLAW

SERVES 4–6

This is my favorite side dish in this book. The crisp and tangy apples are dressed in a homemade coleslaw dressing made with poppy seeds and complemented with cilantro, carrots, and scallions. Double this recipe if you love coleslaw. You will undoubtedly want seconds! (Pictured on page 36 with Easy Fried Fish.)

2 Tbsp. rice vinegar

½ cup mayonnaise

3 Tbsp. honey

1 (1-lb.) bag coleslaw (shredded cabbage and carrots mix) or 1 medium cabbage, shredded, and 2 carrots, julienned

3 scallions, sliced thinly

1 Fuji apple, sliced thinly

¼ cup fresh cilantro, chopped

2 Tbsp. poppy seeds

fresh cracked black pepper, to taste

In a small bowl whisk together the rice vinegar, mayonnaise, and honey until smooth. Set aside. In a large serving bowl, add the coleslaw, scallions, apple slices, and fresh cilantro. Pour in coleslaw dressing and toss until evenly coated. Sprinkle with poppy seeds and pepper. Toss again. Chill 1 hour and serve cold.

ASIAN CARROT SLAW

SERVES 4-6

A light and freshly made carrot slaw with Asian flair. It's semi-sweet with the clean, crisp taste of cilantro and scallions. Serve this side dish with any Asian-inspired main entree to really satisfy your taste buds. (Pictured with Sticky Soy Chicken.)

1 (10-oz.) bag shredded carrots (match stix or julienne)

1 Tbsp. granulated sugar

2 Tbsp. rice vinegar

1 Tbsp. cider vinegar

1 tsp. water

½ Tbsp. sesame oil

½ cup fresh cilantro, chopped

¼ cup scallions, sliced thinly

Place shredded carrots in a medium bowl. In a separate bowl, combine remaining ingredients with a wire whisk except for the cilantro and scallions. Combine well. Pour mixture over carrots and toss to combine. Toss in cilantro and scallions until combined. Chill until ready to serve. Best served cold.

JALAPEÑO CRANBERRY SALSA

SERVES 4-6

I first made this side dish to go with a ham for Christmas dinner, but it's so delightfully fresh and flavorful that now I serve it with chicken or turkey throughout the entire year. If you like spicy and sweet, this side dish will rock your world. Try it on top of meat instead of gravy or even serve it with tortilla chips. (Pictured with Ultimate Slow Cooker Turkey Breast, page 4.)

1½ cups dried cranberries

1 cup orange juice

1 cucumber

1 cup fresh cilantro, chopped

¼ cup lime juice

1 tsp. cumin

1 garlic clove, minced

1 jalapeño, chopped

¼ cup white onion, diced

½ tsp. salt

In a large bowl, add cranberries and orange juice. Set aside. Peel cucumber and cut in half. With a small spoon, gently scoop out the seeds. Slice the cucumber halves into strips and then dice. Place in bowl.

Add cilantro, lime juice, cumin, garlic, jalapeño, onion, and salt. Mix thoroughly and chill for at least 1 hour before serving.

MAKE AHEAD: This is one of those recipes that tastes even better the next day. As with any salsa, the longer the fresh herbs and veggies are allowed to meld, the better. Prepare the night before as a nice time-saver.

SWEET HUSH PUPPIES

SERVES 4-6

Hush puppies always remind me of seafood restaurants. I serve these with my Easy Fried Fish (page 37).

1½ cups flour

1½ cups cornmeal

2 Tbsp. baking powder

2 Tbsp. sugar

1 Tbsp. baking soda

2 tsp. salt

½ tsp. cayenne pepper

1¼ cups buttermilk

2 eggs

1 large yellow onion, grated

Whisk together flour, cornmeal, baking powder, sugar, baking soda, salt, and cayenne pepper in a large bowl. Stir together buttermilk, eggs, and grated onion in a medium bowl. Pour over dry ingredients and stir together until just combined. Set aside to rest for 1 hour.

Pour vegetable oil to a depth of 2 inches in a 6-quart Dutch oven and heat over medium-high heat until a deep-fry thermometer reads 350 degrees. Using a tablespoon, drop small rounds of batter into the oil, making sure to not crowd the pan. Cook, stirring occasionally and flipping halfway through, until golden on the outside and crisp, 3–4 minutes. Remove hush puppies from the oil and drain on paper towels.

FARM FRESH FRUIT SALAD

SERVES 6-8

Farm Fresh Fruit Salad is a light and refreshing summer side dish that is a hit every time I serve it to my guests or family. You can customize this recipe by using your favorite fruit and berries and swapping out the apricot nectar in the dressing for guava, papaya, or peach nectars.

½ cups sugar

1 Tbsp. cornstarch

1½ tsp. pure vanilla extract

1 (10-oz.) can apricot nectar

3 red apples, chopped (I prefer Gala)

2 firm bananas, sliced

2 cups green grapes

2 cups strawberries, sliced

1 pint blueberries

2 cups chopped cantaloupe

handful of fresh mint, chopped

In a microwave safe bowl, whisk together sugar, cornstarch, vanilla, and apricot nectar. Microwave on high for 2 minutes. Whisk again and microwave for another minute. Set aside and let cool slightly.

In a large serving bowl, add prepared fruit and mint. Toss gently with apricot dressing and chill for 1 hour. Serve cold.

ASHLYNN'S AMBROSIA SALAD

SERVES 4–6

1 (20-oz.) can pineapple chunks or tidbits, drained

1 (11-oz.) can mandarin oranges, drained

1 (8-oz.) container sour cream

1 cup cool whip

1 (10.5-oz.) pkg. mini marshmallows

2 cups sweetened flaked coconut

fresh mint sprigs for garnish, if desired

Combine fruit in a large bowl. Stir in sour cream and cool whip until blended. Gently fold in marshmallows and coconut. Cover and chill for 4–6 hours or overnight. Add fresh mint sprigs if desired.

SWEET CORN PUDDING

SERVES 4-6

There is something about sweet corn pudding that screams summer in the South. Maybe it's the simplicity of the recipe and the fact that it goes well with anything grilled. I even like to eat it with my iced tea on the deck. It's the perfect summer side dish.

3 cups canned sweet corn

4 tsp. sugar

6 eggs, lightly beaten

2 cups milk

1 tsp. salt

½ tsp. fresh cracked black pepper

Preheat oven to 350 degrees. In a large bowl, whisk all ingredients together until well mixed. Pour into a buttered 8 × 10 casserole dish. Bake for 30–40 minutes or until firm to the touch and lightly golden brown on the edges. Check to see if it's done by sticking a toothpick in the center. If it comes out clean, it's ready.

MOM'S SWEET SAUSAGE BAKED BEANS

SERVES 6-8

This is one of my mom's best recipes and one we still make today over and over again. It's the perfect side dish to a BBQ dinner and always requested for potlucks.

1 small white onion, chopped

1 tube of Jimmy Dean® sausage, hot flavor

2 (28-oz.) cans Bush's® Southern Pit Barbecue Grillin' Beans® or your favorite baked beans

2 Tbsp. dry mustard

¼ cup molasses

½ cup light brown sugar

Preheat oven to 350 degrees. Cook onions and sausage together in large skillet until sausage is browned and onions are translucent. In a 9 × 13 or larger casserole dish, pour both cans of beans and add the remaining ingredients. With a wooden spoon, gently combine. Add sausage and onion mixture and stir.

Bake in oven uncovered for 30 minutes or until bubbly and slightly browned on top.

N O T E : You can adjust the flavors. If you prefer more heat, add crushed red pepper flakes. Or if you prefer a richer version, add more molasses and sugar.

COUNTRY FRIED APPLES

SERVES 4

This side dish is a wonderful accompaniment to Simple Skillet Pork Chops (page 8). The apples are cooked in a buttery syrup that makes them sweet and tart and tastes just like apple pie filling.

2 Tbsp. butter

4 apples, preferably green, peeled and sliced

⅓ cup brown sugar

1 tsp. cinnamon

In a medium saucepan, heat butter. Once hot, add apple slices, butter, and sugar. Toss until butter is melted and apples are fully coated with sugar and cinnamon. This should take 6–8 minutes. The mixture will turn syrupy and thicken while coating the apples beautifully. Serve warm or room temperature.

FRESH HOT SALSA

SERVES 6-8

This salsa recipe was introduced to me by my friend Dani. When she first brought it over to a party I was having, I couldn't stop eating it. It was the best salsa I had ever tasted and I couldn't believe how easy it was to make using only fresh ingredients. If you are watching your salt intake, reduce the amount in this recipe. Serve with lime tortilla chips. Goes great with Layered Mexican Casserole (page 63).

---

4 large ripe tomatoes

1 jalapeño pepper (with seeds if you like your salsa hot)

2 Tbsp. salt

1 cup (or handful) fresh cilantro, washed

1 large garlic clove

½ large yellow or white onion

Place tomatoes in a large pot, and add water until just covering tomatoes. Boil 5 minutes or until skin on tomatoes start to flake off and peel. In a blender, blend the other five ingredients. Add tomatoes to the mixture in the blender, and blend until all ingredients are combined.

PARMIGIANO-REGGIANO BABY RED POTATOES

SERVES 4-6

There is nothing better than a delicious side dish made with just a few ingredients. I like to serve roasted potatoes with any chicken or beef main entree. If you can't find the Parmigiano-Reggiano cheese blend called for in this recipe, simply substitute for freshly grated Parmesan cheese.

2 lbs. red potatoes, halved

drizzle of extra virgin olive oil

1 cup shredded Parmigiano-Reggiano cheese blend

½ tsp. salt

½ tsp. garlic salt

1 tsp. Italian seasoning

Preheat oven to 400 degrees. Place potatoes on a large cookie sheet. Drizzle with oil and toss with your hands to saturate all sides of potatoes. Sprinkle with remaining ingredients and toss again. Place each potato cut side up and sprinkle with cheese and salt.

Roast potatoes for 40 minutes or until cheese is lightly golden and melted and potatoes are soft when pricked with a fork. Serve hot and add more cheese if desired.

FLUFFY MASHED POTATOES

SERVES 4-6

The simplicity of mashed potatoes makes them a winner in my book. This timeless recipe can be modified in both taste and texture. Add more or less milk depending on the desired consistency, and adjust the salt and fresh cracked black pepper to your liking.

4 lbs. russet potatoes, peeled and quartered

2 sticks butter, at room temperature

salt and fresh cracked black pepper, to taste

1 cup whole milk

1 cup half-and-half

Peel potatoes and cut into fourths. In a large stockpot, bring 5 quarts water to a boil. You only need enough water to cover potatoes. Add a pinch of salt to water. Add potatoes and cook until completely tender, about 15 minutes.

Drain potatoes in colander. Transfer back to stockpot. Add butter, salt, and fresh cracked black pepper. Use a potato masher to mash potatoes. Add milk and half-and-half. Continue mashing and mixing until potatoes are well blended and fluffy. Season to taste with salt and fresh cracked black pepper. Keep warm until ready to serve.

HOMEMADE CAESAR SALAD

SERVES 6-8

Years ago for Thanksgiving, I was given the task of bringing the salad. Caesar salad is my favorite, so I decided to try making my own Caesar dressing. It was such a hit that it has been on our Thanksgiving table every year since.

DRESSING

½ cup extra virgin olive oil

3 Tbsp. lemon juice

4 tsp. anchovy paste

2 Tbsp. Worcestershire sauce

¼ tsp. salt

1 tsp. ground mustard

1 garlic clove, minced

SALAD

10 cups romaine, torn into bite-size pieces or 1 bag

1 cup garlic flavored croutons

½ cup shredded Parmesan cheese

fresh cracked black pepper

Using a wire whisk, mix together dressing ingredients in a large salad bowl. If using a wooden bowl, rub bowl with half a garlic clove in addition to the garlic called for in recipe.

Add romaine and toss until coated. Sprinkle with croutons, cheese, and fresh cracked black pepper. Toss and serve.

SHRIMP CEVICHE

SERVES 4-6

Sometimes appetizers can serve as a side, especially when they're as hearty and full of flavor as this delicious shrimp ceviche. Typically in ceviche, the shrimp is "cooked" while marinating in the lime juice, but I used precooked shrimp to cut down on time. This is a fresh summer side dish that goes great with the Big Flavor Hoisin Burgers (page 71).

3 lbs. cooked shrimp, peeled, deveined and chopped in half

1½ cups lime juice

5 roma tomatoes, diced small

1 large white onion, diced small

1 cup fresh cilantro, rinsed and chopped

⅓ cup Worcestershire sauce

⅓ cup cocktail sauce

2 Tbsp. hot sauce

salt and fresh cracked black pepper, to taste

1 ripe avocado, peeled, pitted, and diced

lime-flavored tortilla chips

In a large bowl, gently mix all ingredients except for the avocado and tortilla chips. Add avocado and toss gently. Adjust the taste with additional salt and fresh cracked black pepper and hot sauce. If too spicy, add more lime juice. Cover and refrigerate at least one hour to give the flavors a chance to meld and to better flavor the shrimp. Serve with lime-flavored tortilla chips.

TENDER GARLIC GREEN BEANS

SERVES 4-6

I make this recipe quite often. It's the fastest and most delicious green bean side dish I have ever had. You'll be amazed how using fresh green beans makes all the difference in the world.

---

3 lbs. green beans, trimmed

3 large garlic cloves, thinly sliced

3 Tbsp. extra virgin olive oil, divided

1 tsp. salt, divided

½ tsp. fresh cracked black pepper, divided

2 Tbsp. fresh parsley, chopped

Cook beans in boiling salted water, covered 5 minutes or until tender. Drain well.

Cook half of garlic in 1 tablespoon oil in a Dutch oven over medium heat for 1 minute or until golden. Add half of beans, and sprinkle with ½ teaspoon salt and ¼ teaspoon pepper. Cook, stirring constantly, 3 minutes. Transfer to a serving dish. Repeat procedure with remaining garlic, oil, beans, salt, and fresh cracked black pepper.

PERFECT POTATO SALAD

SERVES 6-8

This recipe is one of my mom's fabulous side dish recipes and the name says it all. With just a few simple ingredients, it's a cinch to make and tastes creamy and light with just the right amount of dill. We like to keep the potatoes chunky. With just a sprinkle of sea salt and fresh cracked black pepper, it truly is the perfect potato salad.

2 lbs. small red potatoes, quartered

1 cup mayonnaise

½ cup sour cream

2 Tbsp. fresh dill, minced

sea salt and fresh cracked black pepper, to taste

In a large stockpot, boil the potatoes until tender, 15 minutes. Drain in colander and cool slightly.

In a large bowl, mix mayonnaise, sour cream, and dill until combined. Add potatoes, and with a large spoon, toss to coat. Sprinkle with sea salt and fresh cracked black pepper and gently mix.

Refrigerate at least one hour before serving.

MOM'S MACARONI SALAD

SERVES 6-8

I grew up with this side dish as a staple to backyard barbecues. It's now my daughter Ashlynn's favorite recipe. She always asks Grammy to put some aside for her "without the olives" when she makes a batch. If you like Spanish olives, I suggest leaving them in. It's super delicious!

---

1 (1-lb.) box elbow macaroni, prepared according to box directions

1 cup mayonnaise

½ cup sour cream

4 hard-boiled eggs, divided (two thinly sliced and two diced)

¼ cup white onion, diced

½ cup green pepper, diced

1 (8-oz.) jar Spanish olives with pimento, reserving juice

½ tsp. celery seed

1–2 tsp. paprika for garnish

In a small bowl, mix mayonnaise, sour cream, and ¼ cup olive juice from jar. In a large bowl, add cooked elbow macaroni, ¾ cup olives, diced hard-boiled eggs, and celery seed. Gently toss to combine. Transfer to a large serving bowl and decorate the top with thinly sliced eggs (I use an egg slicer) and a handful of olives. Sprinkle with paprika.

FAMILY FAVORITE
DESSERTS

*Save room for dessert and fall in love with Buttercream
Bakehouse's sinfully sweet desserts that will end any
meal with a satisfied sweet tooth.*

ITALIAN CREAM CAKE

SERVES 6-8

A classic dessert and one of my favorites. This tender cake is moist and delicious. It's filled and topped with coconut, pecans, and slathered in a fluffy, sweet cream cheese frosting sprinkled with toasted coconut and additional pecans. A real after-dinner treat.

2 cup flour

1 tsp. baking soda

½ tsp. baking powder

1 cup butter, softened

1½ cup sugar

½ cup light brown sugar

2 tsp. pure vanilla extract

½ tsp. pure almond extract

5 large eggs, room temperature

1 cup buttermilk, room temperature

2 cups sweetened flaked coconut, divided

2 cups pecan pieces, divided

CREAM CHEESE FROSTING

1 (8-oz.) pkg. cream cheese, softened

1 cup butter, softened

4 cups powdered sugar

2 tsp. pure vanilla extract

½ tsp. pure almond extract

4 Tbsp. whole milk

TOPPING
1 cup coconut, toasted

1 cup crushed pecans

Preheat oven to 350 degrees. Butter and flour (or use baking spray) two 8-inch round cake pans. Set aside. Sift the flour, baking soda, and baking powder together. In the bowl of an electric mixer, beat butter, sugar, brown sugar, and extracts on medium speed until light and fluffy, about 3 minutes. Add the eggs one at a time, beating well after each addition and scraping down bowl with a rubber spatula. Add the dry ingredients alternately with the buttermilk, starting and ending with dry ingredients. After all has been added, scrape down bowl and beat on medium-high until just combined. Do not overmix. Stir in 1 cup coconut and 1 cup pecans. Divide the batter evenly between prepared cake pans. Bake for 25–30 minutes until a toothpick inserted into the center comes out clean. Cool completely on a cooling rack.

FOR FROSTING
In the bowl of an electric mixer, beat cream cheese and butter on medium speed until light and fluffy, about 5 minutes. Scrape down bowl with a spatula to ensure all is thoroughly beaten. Add powdered sugar ½ cup at a time on low speed. Increase speed after each addition for one minute. Repeat until all sugar is incorporated. Stir in extracts until combined. Add milk if too thick; add more sugar if not sweet enough or too thin.

TOPPING
Toast remaining coconut by placing in saucepan on stove on medium heat. Stir constantly until coconut is light golden brown with some still white.

To assemble cake, place bottom layer of cake on a cake stand or serving dish. Add about ½ cup of frosting to center of cake and, using a spatula, spread evenly to edge of cake. Top with second layer of cake and continue to frost the top and sides of cake with remaining frosting. Press coconut and pecans on sides and top of cake until completely covered.

NOTE: For easy clean up, place cake stand with frosted cake on a cookie sheet when adding coconut to top and sides of cake.

CHOCOLATE SILK PIE

SERVES 4-6

A sinfully rich and smooth chocolate silk pie made extra fluffy and creamy with dark chocolate, cream cheese, and Cool Whip. Using a premade chocolate cookie crust makes this recipe simple and quick.

---

1 (12-oz.) package dark chocolate chips, melted and divided

1 (8-oz.) pkg. cream cheese, softened

1 tsp. vanilla extract

2 cups Cool Whip or fresh whipped cream

1 (8-in.) premade chocolate cookie crust

In a microwave-safe bowl, melt chocolate chips on medium-high heat for one minute. Stir and microwave again for 1 more minute, and stir again. Be careful not to burn the chocolate. If the chocolate is not fully melted, microwave again for 10 seconds and stir vigorously until smooth and melted. Set aside.

In an electric mixer, beat cream cheese and vanilla until light and fluffy, 3 minutes. Reserve ¼ cup of chocolate for drizzling on top of pie. Pour remaining chocolate into mixing bowl with cream cheese, and beat on low until combined. Add Cool Whip and beat on low for 2 minutes, or until fully combined. Pour into cookie crust. Top with remaining cool whip. Using a spoon, dip into remaining melted chocolate and drizzle over pie. Refrigerate at least 4 hours before serving.

SOUTHERN RED VELVET CAKE TRIFLE

SERVES 6-8

This delectable dessert is great for a crowd. It's pleasing to the eye with its colorful mix of red velvet cake, coconut, blueberries, and cream cheese frosting.

2½ cups flour

1 tsp. baking soda

2½ tsp. cocoa

1½ cups sugar

2 eggs

1½ cups canola oil or vegetable oil

1 tsp. vinegar

1 (1-oz.) bottle red food coloring

1 tsp. pure vanilla extract

1 cup buttermilk, room temperature

CREAM CHEESE FROSTING

1 cup unsalted butter

1 (8-oz.) pkg. cream cheese

4 cups powdered sugar, sifted

1 tsp. vanilla

dash of salt

TOPPING

1 cup of sweetened shredded coconut

1 cup fresh blueberries (if desired)

sprig of mint (if desired)

Preheat oven to 350 degrees. Grease and flour a 10-inch round cake pan.

Sift flour, baking soda, and cocoa together. In a separate large bowl, beat sugar and eggs together.

In a separate bowl, mix together oil, vinegar, food coloring, and vanilla. Add to the bowl of eggs and sugar and beat until combined. Alternate the flour mixture and the buttermilk to the wet mixture. Start and end with the flour.

Pour batter into pan. Tap the pan on counter to level out the batter and release air bubbles. Bake for 25 minutes or until a toothpick inserted near the middle comes out clean. Be careful not to overbake or you'll have a dry cake.

Let cake cool on a wire rack for 10 minutes before turning out of pan. Cool completely.

FOR FROSTING

In the bowl of an electric mixer, beat butter and cream cheese well, about 5 minutes. Add sugar ½ cup at a time, beating on high speed after each addition. Repeat until all sugar is added. Stir in vanilla and a dash of salt. Switch to a paddle attachment and beat on medium for another 2 minutes or until all the air bubbles are gone and the frosting is smooth.

FOR COMBINING INTO TRIFLE

When cake is cooled, cut into 1-inch cubes. Layer in bottom of trifle bowl. Add 2 cups frosting with a large spoon. Smooth gently with the back of spoon. You may also pipe the frosting into the trifle bowl for a neater appearance. Repeat with more cake and frosting, ending with a layer of frosting. Top with coconut, fresh blueberries, and a sprig of mint.

LEMONY PEACH PIE BUNDT CAKE

SERVES 6-8

Sometimes you just need something simple to throw together and a doctored cake mix recipe is the perfect way to go. Jazz up a boxed lemon cake mix with a few simple ingredients and a can of peach pie filling. Pour into a Bundt cake pan for a stunning, easy-to-prepare delicious dessert that you can whip up on the fly.

---

1 box lemon cake mix (I used Betty Crocker®)

1 cup water

4 eggs

½ cup sugar

1 cup flour

¼ cup vegetable oil

½ tsp. lemon emulsion (or pure lemon extract)

1 tsp. Tahitian vanilla extract (or pure vanilla extract)

1 (21-oz.) can peach pie filling

powdered sugar, for dusting

Preheat oven to 350 degrees. Spray Bundt pan with baking spray. Sprinkle pan with some sugar.

Add all ingredients except for the pie filling and mix with electric mixer on medium speed for two minutes. Empty pie filling in a small bowl and break up the peach pieces. Stir into the batter and fill prepared pan.

Bake for 35 minutes on center rack until toothpick inserted in cake comes out clean.

Cool for 25 minutes or until completely cooled. Sprinkle with powdered sugar.

DARK CHOCOLATE CHIP WALNUT COOKIE BARS

SERVES 4-6

This recipe is a hit in my home. If you love homemade chocolate chip cookies, you'll love this cookie bar recipe. It has the same moistness and soft texture on the inside as a gooey chocolate chip cookie. I used dark chocolate chips but you may use any variety you love best.

½ cup unsalted butter

½ cup shortening

1 cup sugar

1 cup brown sugar

3 eggs

1 tsp. vanilla

2 cups flour

1 cup cake flour

1 tsp. baking soda

1 tsp. salt

2 cups dark chocolate chips

1 cup chopped walnuts

Preheat oven to 375 degrees. Line a small 8 × 8 casserole dish with foil, tightly sealing corners and edges. Spray with baking spray. Set aside.

In the bowl of an electric mixer, beat butter and shortening for two minutes on high speed until light and fluffy. Add sugars and beat until combined, scraping down sides. Add eggs one at a time, beating on low after each addition and scraping down edges. Add vanilla and stir.

In a separate bowl, sift dry ingredients. Add dry ingredients to butter and sugar mixture and mix on low until just combined. Do not overmix. Add chocolate chips and walnuts and stir with a spoon to combine. Using a flat-cake spatula, gently spread cookie dough into prepared baking dish until even.

Bake for 30 minutes. Turn heat down to 325 degrees and bake for another 25–30 minutes. If edges are getting too golden brown, cover them with foil and continue baking. It's okay if it seems slightly undercooked in the center—this will give you a super soft, chewy texture that tastes amazing. Just be sure the center is somewhat firm and not overly soft before removing from oven.

BOURBON PEACH RASPBERRY COBBLER

SERVES 6-8

Bourbon and peaches is a match made in heaven. The bourbon brings out the peachy flavor, adding a sophisticated note to this sweet, rich dessert with raspberries and traditional oat cobbler topping. Serve warm with a scoop of vanilla ice cream for a sinfully delicious indulgence.

5 ripe peaches, sliced

1 (6-oz.) container fresh raspberries

½ cup bourbon

⅓ cup sugar

¼ tsp. nutmeg

2 Tbsp. cornstarch

1 tsp. cinnamon

1 tsp. vanilla

TOPPING

1 cup flour

1 cup rolled quick cooking oats

⅓ cup sugar

2 sticks butter

1 tsp. cinnamon

¼ cup brown sugar

vanilla ice cream, if desired

Preheat oven to 375 degrees. In a large bowl, add first 8 ingredients. Toss gently to coat fruit until mixture is well combined.

In a separate bowl, combine topping ingredients. Using a pastry blender or two forks in a crisscross motion, blend ingredients until completely combined.

Add peach mixture to an 8 × 8 baking dish or a 8- or 10-inch cast iron skillet.

Evenly place topping mixture and bake uncovered for 30 minutes. Serve warm with ice cream if desired.

SUGAR COOKIE APPLE CRISP

SERVES 6-8

Just when you thought apple crisp couldn't get any better, it just did! Lightly spiced, sweet, juicy apples are baked with a soft and chewy sugar cookie crust on top. You'll never bake apple crisp the old way again.

6 large Granny Smith apples, peeled and coarsely chopped (3 cups)

½ cup sugar

⅓ cup brown sugar

1 tsp. ground cinnamon

¼ tsp. nutmeg

¼ cup walnuts, chopped

½ stick butter, cut into small cubes

1 tube of prepared sugar cookie dough at room temperature

Heat oven to 325 degrees. Spray bottom and sides of 2-quart casserole dish with baking spray. In large bowl, gently toss apples, sugar, brown sugar, cinnamon, and nutmeg until combined. Spread mixture in casserole dish and top evenly with walnuts and cubed butter.

With a spoon, scoop a tablespoon of cookie dough and add evenly to top of apple mixture. With the back of the spoon, flatten cookie dough scoops, so that they spread slightly and touch. The cookie dough doesn't need to reach the sides of pan.

Bake 45–55 minutes or until apples are bubbly and sugar cookie is baked through and lightly golden on top. Serve warm.

COMPANY'S COMING RASPBERRY TRIFLE

SERVES 6-8

My mom has been making this trifle recipe for years. I remember as a kid thinking it was a grown-up dessert because of the distinct taste of sherry soaked in the ladyfingers. Now, as an adult, I describe this dessert as nothing short of sophisticated and sinful.

---

2 (3-oz.) packages ladyfingers cookies, separated

¼ cup sherry liquor

3¼ oz. box vanilla instant pudding mix

2 cups cold whole milk

1 cup heavy cream

1 cup raspberry jam

2 (6-oz.) containers fresh raspberries

1 cup thin sliced almonds

On a cookie sheet, lay out the ladyfingers so that they aren't touching. Sprinkle the ladyfingers with sherry. Arrange half of the ladyfingers in the bottom of a 14-cup glass trifle bowl. They should cover bottom of bowl.

Prepare pudding mix with the milk as package directs. In the bowl of an electric mixer, beat the heavy cream until stiff peaks form. Fold the cream into the pudding.

Warm jam by microwaving in a small bowl at 10-second intervals, stirring often until loose and slightly thinned. Sprinkle ½ cup warmed jam over prepared ladyfingers. Top jam with half of fresh raspberries. Layer with half of pudding and half of nuts. Repeat layers reserving a few raspberries and nuts for garnish.

Cover and chill at least 4 hours to give ladyfingers a chance to soften and the flavors to meld. Serve chilled.

GRANDMA'S COCONUT RICE PUDDING

SERVES 4-6

My maternal grandmother was the best cook. She never wrote down her recipes, but I think I nailed this one pretty darn good, if I do say so myself. This is not your typical rice pudding. The incredible flavor comes from simmering instant rice (a time saver) in a cream of coconut broth spiced with anise seed, ginger, cinnamon, and nutmeg. It's the most unique and creamiest rice pudding you'll ever try.

1½ cups cream of coconut

1 (8-oz.) can evaporated milk

3 cups of whole milk

3–5 medium to large sticks of cinnamon

1 Tbsp. anise seed

1 Tbsp. whole cloves

1 small-medium piece whole fresh ginger, peeled

2 cups instant rice, uncooked

⅓ cup of granulated sugar

¾ cup raisins

½ tsp. salt

1 cup water

1 tsp. cinnamon

In a large saucepan, simmer the first 7 ingredients on low heat for 20 minutes, stirring occasionally. Do not boil.

Drain broth through a sieve or strainer over a large stockpot. Place the cinnamon sticks back in the broth. These will stay in the pot and cook with the remaining ingredients until the rice pudding is finished.

Add remaining ingredients to the broth except for the water and cinnamon. Raise heat to medium-high and boil for 40 minutes, stirring constantly. Lower heat to medium if the mixture begins to rise in pan. The mixture will begin to thicken as it cooks.

Add 1 cup of water after 20 minutes or when the mixture is very thick. Stir and bring back to a boil for the remainder of the cooking time, about 20 minutes or until the pudding is thick. It should have a pudding consistency and the rice should be cooked thoroughly.

Add cinnamon and stir. Pour in individual serving dishes and refrigerate until completely cooled 20 minutes.

Sprinkle with a dash more cinnamon for garnish. Serve cold.

BAILEYS® BROWNIES

SERVES 4-6

A decadent dessert doesn't have to take a lot of effort or skill to make. Using a brownie mix makes this recipe a fast and easy favorite at the Bakehouse. Adding Bailey's to the batter gives it amazing flavor and makes this a super indulgent treat.

BROWNIE

1 box brownie mix

½ cup Baileys® Original Irish Cream

½ cup oil

3 eggs

FROSTING

1 (8-oz.) pkg. cream cheese, room temperature

½ stick unsalted butter, room temperature

3 cups powdered sugar

3–4 Tbsp. Baileys® Original Irish Cream

1 tsp. vanilla extract

Heat oven to 350 degrees. Grease the bottom of a 8 × 8 baking dish. In large bowl, combine all brownie ingredients and beat for 50 strokes with a spoon. Spread evenly in greased pan.

Bake for 30–35 minutes or until toothpick inserted in the center of brownies comes out clean. Do not overbake. Cool completely before frosting. Once cooled, frost brownies evenly using a cake spatula.

FOR FROSTING

In a large mixing bowl, beat cream cheese and butter with an electric mixer until light and fluffy, or 5 minutes. Add sugar 1 cup at a time while beating on low speed and scraping down sides of bowl after each addition. Add Baileys Irish cream and vanilla, and beat on low until combined, 1 minute.

ABOUT THE AUTHOR

Dina Foglio Crowell is a proud mom, professional food blogger, food stylist, photographer, and author. She is the talent and photographer behind the popular baking blog Buttercream Bakehouse and author of cookbook *Delicious Mornings,* published by Cedar Fort Publishing in 2014. She has appeared on the national syndicated talk show at KABC *Food and Wine with Chef Jamie.* She has also appeared on *Problems & Solutions with Cathy Blythe,* a daily talk show which originates in Lincoln, Nebraska, and is syndicated on a network of stations in Nebraska, South Dakota, Minnesota, and Iowa.

Dina has always had a passion for baking. In 2009 she started a home-based cake decorating business called Buttercream. She soon became an award-winning master cake decorator with two wins in the National Capital Area Cake Show. She discovered blogging as a way to share her recipes and baking knowledge with other home-bakers and cake enthusiasts. Her blog, Buttercream Bakehouse, grew quickly in popularity and became her full-time passion when she closed the doors to her cake business in 2010.

As Dina honed her talents for food photography and recipe development, she was accepted by dozens of ad networks including Pollinate Media Group, Collective Bias, and Tap Influence. She became a professional

blogger and brand ambassador, creating recipes and marketing campaigns for well-known brands including Hershey's®, Nestle®, Kraft Foods®, and Betty Crocker®, just to name a few.

A foodie at heart, Dina also serves as a volunteer field editor for *Taste of Home* magazine and is listed as a favorite blogger at tasteofhome.com.

The consummate professional at work is an everyday occurrence. Producing and developing a spectacular cookbook to inspire "the everyday cook and baker" is no easy feat, but a true labor of love.

Her first cookbook, *Delicious Mornings,* was the #1 new breakfast cookbook release on Amazon for both November and December 2014. Over a 1000 copies sold in independent bookstores, Barnes and Noble, Books-a-Million, and Amazon in just a few short months. You can also find Dina in the June/July 2015 issue of *Simple and Delicious,* a *Taste of Home* magazine. She was named "recipe star" for her recipe for birthday cake pancakes featured in the magazine.

Dina's parents, Lucy and Jimmy Foglio, are her biggest supporters and have always been her rock. Her children, Tristen, Ashlynn, Kayeden, and Brennen, and two Maltese, Ollie and Finn, keep her strong, motivated, and focused on loving life, counting her blessings, and living her dream.

SCAN TO VISIT

WWW.BUTTERCREAM-BAKEHOUSE.COM